What's in
Daily Math Practice

P9-DBQ-874

36 Weekly Sections

Monday through Thursday

- two computation problems

  During the first 18 weeks, the computation problems are organized as follows:
  - Monday–addition
  - Tuesday–subtraction
  - Wednesday–multiplication
  - Thursday–division

  During the second 18 weeks (weeks 19–36), the computation problems are presented in random order.

- two items that practice a variety of math skills

- one word problem

Friday

Friday's format includes one problem that is more extensive and may require multiple steps. These problems emphasize reasoning and communication in mathematics.

Also featured on Friday is a graph form where students record the number of problems they got correct each day that week.

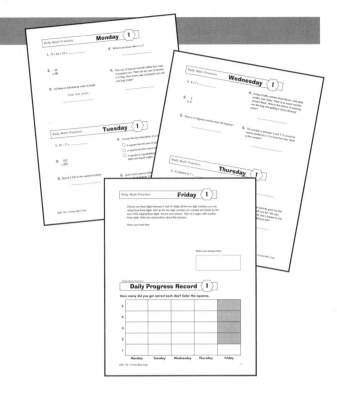

Additional Features

Scope and Sequence

Scope and sequence charts on pages 3 and 4 detail the specific skills to be practiced and show when they will be presented. The skills included are found in math texts at this level.

Answer Key

The answer key begins on page 117.

How to Solve Word Problems Chart

Award Certificate

How to Use Daily Math Practice

You may want to use all of the following presentations throughout the year to keep each lesson fresh and interesting.

1. Make overhead transparencies of the lessons. Present each lesson as an oral activity with the entire class. Write answers and make corrections using an erasable marker.

   As the class becomes more familiar with *Daily Math Practice*, you may want students to mark their answers first and then check them against correct responses marked on the transparency.

2. Reproduce the pages for individuals or partners to work on independently. Check answers as a group, using an overhead transparency to model the correct answers. (Use these pages as independent practice only after much oral group experience with the lessons.)

3. Occasionally you may want to use a day's or even a full week's lesson(s) as a test to see how individuals are progressing in their acquisition of skills.

Some Important Considerations

1. Allow students to use whatever tools they need to solve problems. Some students will choose to use manipulatives, while others will want to make drawings.

2. It is important that students be able to share their solutions. This modeling of a variety of problem-solving techniques provides a great learning benefit. Don't scrimp on the amount of time you allow for discussing how solutions were reached.

3. With the focus of the first four days being on computation and problem solving, it is recommended that calculators be used only on Fridays, when the focus is much more detailed, with less emphasis on computation. In some instances, however, you may want to allow the use of calculators to solve the daily word problems.

Suggestions and Options

1. Sometimes you will not have taught a given skill before it appears in a lesson. These items should then be done together. Tell the class that you are going to work on a skill they have not yet been taught. Use the practice time to conduct a minilesson on that skill.

2. Customize the daily lessons to the needs of your class.

   • If there are skills that are not included in the grade-level expectancies of the particular program you teach, you may choose to skip those items.

   • If you feel your class needs more practice than is provided, add these "extras" on your own in the form of a one-item warm-up or posttest.

3. Many of the Friday problems are quite challenging and lend themselves to partner or small-group collaboration.

EMC 754 • © Evan-Moor Corp.

Week	1	2	3	4	5	6	7	8	9	10	11	12	13	14	15	16	17	18	19	20	21	22	23	24	25	26	27	28	29	30	31	32	33	34	35	36
Numbers																																				
base-ten system			●					●																●			●	●	●		●	●				
word/standard forms				●	●	●			●	●	●									●	●									●					●	
place value	●			●		●			●		●		●								●	●	●						●	●	●			●	●	
rounding		●					●		●		●										●	●						●		●				●		
estimation														●									●			●				●					●	
properties/number relationships					●				●					●		●	●								●				●	●	●			●	●	
factors and GCF					●	●		●											●			●	●	●					●			●				
multiples and LCM							●			●				●									●				●									
equalities/inequalities	●				●	●			●		●								●	●													●			●
decimals				●	●	●		●	●	●	●	●	●	●	●	●	●	●	●	●	●	●	●	●	●	●	●	●	●	●	●	●	●	●	●	●
fractions			●		●	●		●	●	●	●	●	●	●	●	●	●		●	●		●		●	●				●	●	●			●		●
percents							●	●				●										●		●	●			●			●	●				
integers																				●				●	●			●		●	●			●		
exponents					●								●					●		●				●	●			●		●	●		●	●	●	●
prime numbers	●														●													●								
Patterns/Algebra																																				
figural patterns				●				●																												
numerical patterns		●				●				●	●		●				●								●	●	●		●	●		●				●
expressions										●			●				●		●			●				●	●	●		●		●			●	●
function tables												●		●												●						●				
equations		●	●		●						●							●		●			●	●		●					●		●		●	
Geometry/Spatial																																				
2-dimensional shapes	●		●	●					●	●	●	●	●	●			●	●					●		●		●				●		●	●		●
3-dimensional shapes			●						●	●	●	●		●					●										●							
symmetry	●			●																		●														
congruency						●						●														●			●						●	
angle						●											●									●		●	●		●		●	●		●

Week	1	2	3	4	5	6	7	8	9	10	11	12	13	14	15	16	17	18	19	20	21	22	23	24	25	26	27	28	29	30	31	32	33	34	35	36
Measurement																																				
weight	●														●	●	●		●	●				●	●		●		●		●	●	●			
capacity	●		●		●		●								●		●			●										●			●		●	●
time	●		●		●	●	●											●	●		●		●					●	●	●	●	●	●	●	●	●
temperature	●		●									●				●																				
length		●				●		●			●								●			●			●				●	●		●		●	●	
perimeter			●						●						●		●	●				●	●					●		●					●	
area				●	●		●	●	●	●		●				●								●		●				●	●	●		●	●	●
volume								●				●								●																
money	●	●	●	●	●	●	●	●	●	●	●		●	●		●		●		●	●	●		●	●	●	●	●		●	●		●	●		
Data Analysis & Probability																																				
coordinate graphing					●				●											●															●	
constructing graphs			●				●				●		●		●						●															
interpreting graphs/charts														●				●		●							●									
mode, median, mean, range			●				●	●	●				●	●	●	●	●	●		●				●			●				●	●	●			
probability	●			●				●	●	●																										
permutations/combinations																						●												●		

1. $19 + 26 + 23 =$ _688_

2.
$$
\begin{array}{r}
68 \\
+\ 48 \\
\hline
116
\end{array}
$$

3. List these in decreasing order of length.

3 cm, 3 m, 3 mm

3 M, 3 cm, 3 mm

4. What is six hours after 2 P.M.?

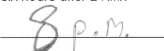 8 P.M.

5. One cup of popcorn kernels makes four cups of popped corn. There are six cups of kernels in a bag. How many cups of popped corn will one bag make?

10 cups

---

1. $56 - 17 =$ _39_

$$
\begin{array}{r}
56 \\
-\ 17 \\
\hline
39
\end{array}
$$

2.
$$
\begin{array}{r}
837 \\
-\ 614 \\
\hline
223
\end{array}
$$

3. Round 5,294 to the nearest hundred.

5,000

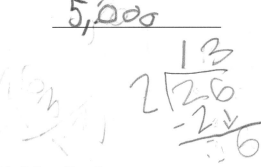

4. Choose the best description of a square.

○ A square has two sets of parallel sides.

○ A square has four equal angles.

⊗ A square is a quadrilateral with equal sides and equal angles.

5. Aunt Carol's peanut brittle recipe calls for $\frac{1}{2}$ pound of peanuts. If she makes 26 batches for the bake sale, how many pounds of peanuts will she use?

1/2 lb = 1 batch
1 = 2 batches   13 pounds

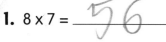

1. 8 x 7 = _56_

2. 9
  x 2
  18

3. What is 12 degrees warmer than 38 degrees?

50 degrees

4. A bag of taffy contains three flavors: chocolate, vanilla, and cherry. There is an equal number of each flavor. What is the chance of reaching into the bag and getting a cherry-flavored piece?

_____

5. The number is between 0 and 9. It cannot be evenly divided by 2. It is more than five. What is the number?

_____

1. 63 divided by 7 = _____

2. 4)28

3. Write this number in standard notation.

three thousand six hundred seventeen

_____

4. What is half of 14?

_____

5. Jill has an old bike. Her parents gave her $40 to repair it. New tires will cost $21. She also wants to buy a bell for $5 and a basket for $13. How much money will Jill have left?

_____

EMC 754 • © Evan-Moor Corp.

Friday ⟨1⟩

Choose any three digits between 0 and 10. Make all the two-digit numbers you can using those three digits. Add up the two-digit numbers you created and divide by the sum of the original three digits. Record your answer. Then do it again with another three digits. Write your observations about the answers.

Show your work here.

Write your answer here.

Daily Progress Record ⟨1⟩

How many did you get correct each day? Color the squares.

	Monday	Tuesday	Wednesday	Thursday	Friday
5					
4					
3					
2					
1					

1. 33 + 22 + 36 = _____

2.   73
    + 89

3. How many inches are in 5 feet?

_____

4. Draw as many lines of symmetry as possible.

5. Wilbur Wright was born in 1867. His brother Orville was born in 1871. How old was each brother in 1903?

_____

How much older was Wilbur than Orville?

_____

---

1. 87 − 38 = _____

2.   398
    − 235

3. Complete this table.

Subjects	Hands
1	2
2	4
3	6
4	
5	
10	
15	

4. Name three common denominators of $\frac{1}{3}$ and $\frac{1}{2}$.

_____

5. Mercury is 58 million kilometers from the sun. Earth is 150 million kilometers from the sun. How much farther from the sun is Earth?

_____

EMC 754 • © Evan-Moor Corp.

Wednesday ⟨2⟩

1. 5 × 9 = _____

2.   3
      × 8
   ‾‾‾‾‾

3. What comes next?

44 22 88 44 176 88 _____

____   ____

4. Write the factors of 14. Circle the prime factors.

_____

5. The Community Council is replanting six flower boxes downtown. Each flower box holds 32 petunias. If petunias come in packs of 8, how many packs will be needed?

_____

Thursday ⟨2⟩

1. 5)‾35‾

2. 4)‾20‾

3. What place value does the 6 have in 764,328?

_____

4. Fill in the correct symbol.

< = >

31 ◯ 47

5. The coffee shop has nine apple pies cut into fourths. Each piece sells for $1.50. How much are all the pieces worth?

_____

Friday ⟨2⟩

Magic Square

In this magic square, the sum of each row, column, and diagonal is the same. Fill in the squares. Reduce your answers to the lowest terms.

$\frac{1}{4}$	$1\frac{1}{4}$	
$1\frac{7}{12}$		
$\frac{2}{3}$		

Daily Math Practice

Daily Progress Record ⟨2⟩

How many did you get correct each day? Color the squares.

	Monday	Tuesday	Wednesday	Thursday	Friday
5					
4					
3					
2					
1					

EMC 754 • © Evan-Moor Corp.

Monday 3

1. 36 + 10 + 1 + 49 = _____

2. 415
+ 398

3. What is the perimeter of an 8" square?

_____

4. It was 102°F on the Fourth of July. It was 50 degrees cooler on Thanksgiving. What was the temperature on Thanksgiving?

_____

5. Tamara has twelve coins. One-quarter are dimes, one-half are quarters, and the rest are pennies. What is the value of Tamara's money?

_____

Tuesday 3

1. 783 – 388 = _____

2. 85
– 16

3. Construct a graph to show the information below. Use a sheet of graph paper.

Goals Scored	Ducks	Opponents
Game 1	4	2
Game 2	3	0
Game 3	1	5
Game 4	6	3

4. Name two things in your desk that are rectangular prisms.

_____

5. The nature museum is open seven days a week. Every day 105 people come to see the exhibits. How many people come to the museum in one week?

_____

Wednesday ⟨3⟩

1. 3 × 5 = _____

2.   7
       x 4

3. If *a* = 2, what is the value of *a* + 6?

_____

4. If Bert is responsible for mowing 50% of the lawn, what does that mean?

_____

_____

5. If Mario eats two cups of pretzels every night while he watches television, how many cups does he eat in one week?

_____

If there are 13 pretzels in each cup, how many pretzels does he eat?

_____

Thursday ⟨3⟩

1. 3)̄2̄1̄

2. 6)̄3̄0̄

3. Which of these is more?

◯ a liter   ◯ a milliliter

4. What is the mean (average) of this data?

5, 8, 9, 6, 2

_____

5. How many months are there in three years?

_____

EMC 754 • © Evan-Moor Corp.

Friday ⟨3⟩

State the rule and fill in the missing numbers in this chart.

Input	Output
12	10
	16
32	
62	35
70	39
86	

Daily Progress Record ⟨3⟩

How many did you get correct each day? Color the squares.

	Monday	Tuesday	Wednesday	Thursday	Friday
5					
4					
3					
2					
1					

1. 39 + 19 + 17 = _____

2.   4,139
      + 2,524
      _____

3. Correct the mistakes.

1,426 + 2,317 = 3,742

4,138 + 3,522 = 7,663

4. How many sides does a pentagon have?

_____

5. There are 59 boys and 49 girls in the baseball league this year. If there are 9 teams in the league, how many players will each team have?

_____

---

1. 94 – 26 = _____

2.   284
      – 188
      _____

3. What are the next four figures in this pattern?

 ___ ___ ___ ___

4. When you write $3.01, what does the decimal point mean?

_____

_____

_____

5. The number is less than 20. It is an odd one-digit number. It is not the number of sides of a triangle. It can be divided by three. What is the number?

_____

EMC 754 • © Evan-Moor Corp.

1. 5 × 8 = _____

2.   24
      x 2

3. What number sentences can be created using 9, 7, and 16?

_____

_____

4. What place value does the 7 have in 187,300?

_____

5. During batting practice, each player was pitched 12 balls. If 9 players came to practice, how many balls were pitched?

_____

If the players each hit an average of 8 balls, how many balls were hit?

_____

Daily Math Practice

Thursday 4

1. 81 ÷ 9 = _____

2. 3⟌51

3. How many lines of symmetry does a square have?

_____

4. Write this number in standard notation.

twelve thousand twenty

_____

5. Kim's new bike cost twice as much as Yoko's. If Yoko's bike cost $189, how much did Kim's bike cost?

_____

Friday ⟨4⟩

Study the figure below. Then determine its area.

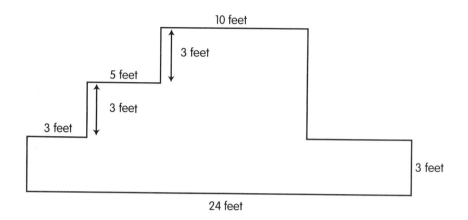

Write your answer here.

Daily Progress Record ⟨4⟩

How many did you get correct each day? Color the squares.

	Monday	Tuesday	Wednesday	Thursday	Friday
5					
4					
3					
2					
1					

EMC 754 • © Evan-Moor Corp.

1. 19 + 27 + 19 + 24 = _____

2. 9,124
+ 6,285

3. What is 13 hours past 1 A.M.?

_____

4. What is the value of *y* in this equation?

$$3 + y = 12$$

_____

5. The bakers made 25 each of lemon, apple, and cherry pies each hour on Monday. If they worked 8 hours, how many pies did they bake altogether?

_____

1. 262 – 127 = _____

2. 488
– 49

3. Plot the points A (4, 1), B (⁻2, 3), and C (3, 0) on this coordinate plane.

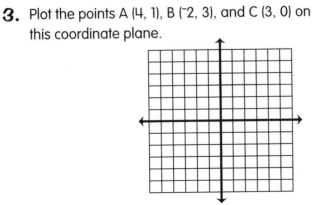

4. How many cups are in a quart?

_____

5. Ted's patio is the shape of a right triangle. Tell how he should determine the area of the patio.

18
7

_____

_____

_____

Wednesday ⟨5⟩

1. $9 \times 7 =$ _____

2. $\begin{array}{r} 3.2 \\ \times\ \ 4 \\ \hline \end{array}$

3. What does 4^3 mean?

_____

4. Fill in the correct symbol.

$<\ =\ >$

$0.4 \bigcirc 0.40$

5. There are 58 stuffed birds in the habitat exhibit. If $\frac{1}{2}$ of the birds are from South America, how many South American birds are there?

_____

Thursday ⟨5⟩

1. $32 \div 8 =$ _____

2. $9\overline{)45}$

3. List all the factors of 6.

_____

4. Write 705 in word form.

_____

5. The diameter of Earth is 12,757 kilometers. The diameter of Saturn is 120,664 kilometers. The diameter of Uranus is 51,499 kilometers. Is the sum of these three planets' diameters more or less than Jupiter's diameter of 142,804 kilometers? By how much?

_____

EMC 754 • © Evan-Moor Corp.

Friday ⬡ 5

Number Puzzles

1. Choose 3 **different** digits from one to nine.
2. Make the largest and the smallest numbers you can using the three digits.
3. Subtract the smaller number from the larger number.
4. Reverse the order of the digits in the answer and add it to step 3's answer.
5. Write the answer.

Try it again with 3 different digits.
Try it with 4 different digits.
How did the answer change from 3 digits to 4 digits?

Do you think that the same thing will happen if you try it with 5 digits?   yes   no
Try it and see.

Daily Math Practice

Daily Progress Record ⬡ 5

How many did you get correct each day? Color the squares.

	Monday	Tuesday	Wednesday	Thursday	Friday
5					
4					
3					
2					
1					

Monday ⟨6⟩

1. $96 + 93 + 98 =$ _____

2. $\begin{array}{r} 649 \\ +\ 79 \\ \hline \end{array}$

3. Fill in the correct symbol.

    < = >

    $0.5 \bigcirc 5$

4. List all the factors of 10.

    _____

5. Carlos does various jobs to earn money. He earned $9.58 by collecting cans and bottles. He earned $18.75 baby-sitting. If he has saved $10.50 of his allowance, how much money does he have now?

    _____

Tuesday ⟨6⟩

1. $949 - 325 =$ _____

2. $\begin{array}{r} 737 \\ -\ 368 \\ \hline \end{array}$

3. Write 132 in word form.

    _____

4. What place value does the 3 have in 8.3?

    _____

5. Ryan has 68 CDs. He can store 15 CDs in a wooden crate. How many crates will he need?

    _____

EMC 754 • © Evan-Moor Corp.

Wednesday 〈 6 〉

1. 3 x 9 = _____

2.   90
    x 5
   ‾‾‾‾‾

3. What are the next three numbers in this pattern?

2, 3, 5, 6, 8, _____, _____, _____

4. Which rectangle is congruent to the first one?

_____

5. Sammie worked in the garden for several hours one Saturday morning. She began at 8:30 A.M. and stopped 3 hours and 40 minutes later. At what time did she stop?

_____

Thursday 〈 6 〉

1. 7)‾49‾

2. 2)‾86‾

3. Order these lengths from shortest to longest.

1 inch   1 foot   10 inches   10 feet   1 yard

_____

4. Which of these angles are less than 90°?

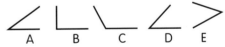

_____

5. Sudi and Tosha are eating pancakes. If they each can eat one pancake in 3 minutes, how long will it take the two of them to eat 10 pancakes?

_____

Sarim has $1 in coins. One-fifth of the coins are dimes, two-fifteenths are nickels, and two-thirds are pennies. Tell how many of each coin he has.

Show your work here.

Write your answer here.

How many did you get correct each day? Color the squares.

	Monday	Tuesday	Wednesday	Thursday	Friday
5					
4					
3					
2					
1					

EMC 754 • © Evan-Moor Corp.

Monday 7

1. 556 + 436 = _____

2.   91.24
      + 62.85

3. What are the first three multiples of 4?

_____

4. Round 6,789 to the nearest hundred.

_____

5. Six boys equally divided the candy in the bowl. Each boy got 3 pieces of taffy, 2 jawbreakers, and 7 mints. How many pieces of candy were in the bowl?

_____

Tuesday 7

1. 5,473 – 4,266 = _____

2.   361
      – 187

3. Construct a graph for this data. Use a sheet of graph paper.

Week	Hot Lunches Purchased
1	638
2	574
3	496
4	584

4. Using the chart in problem 3, what is the average number of hot lunches purchased per week?

_____

5. Mrs. Burns is making cookies. The recipe calls for $3\frac{1}{2}$ cups of flour. If she wants to double the recipe, how much flour does she need?

_____

Wednesday ⟨7⟩

1. 7 x 6 = _____

2.   25
    x 3

3. What is 50% of 76?

_____

4. Order these weights from lightest to heaviest.

    10 ounces   1 pound   1 ounce

_____

5. Gramps has six nickels, one dime, nine pennies, and two quarters in his money pouch. Peg has a dollar bill. Who has more money? By how much?

_____

Thursday ⟨7⟩

1. 6$\overline{)18}$

2. 4$\overline{)32}$

3. How many minutes are in 2 hours and 37 minutes?

_____

4. What is the area of this rectangle?

3 cm

7.5 cm

_____

5. Marilyn's horse eats 12 pounds of food every day. How much food will Marilyn need for the month of January?

_____

  EMC 754 • © Evan-Moor Corp.

Friday 7

Mrs. Sage will print a copy of the class alphabet book for each student. The book is formatted in $\frac{1}{2}$ pages with a title page, a page for each letter, and an end page. If there are 70 students, how many reams of paper will Mrs. Sage need for the books? (1 ream = 500 sheets)

Show your work here.

Write your answer here.

Daily Math Practice

Daily Progress Record 7

How many did you get correct each day? Color the squares.

	Monday	Tuesday	Wednesday	Thursday	Friday
5					
4					
3					
2					
1					

Monday ⟨8⟩

1. 587 + 239 = _____

2.   8,236
       + 1,537
       ‾‾‾‾‾‾‾

3. What is 37% of 100?

_____

4. What is the median of this data?

10, 12, 24, 18, 14, 26, 22

_____

5. Luis is 12" shorter than Eva. Eva is 3" taller than Jose. If Jose is 48" tall, how tall are Eva and Luis?

_____

Tuesday ⟨8⟩

1. 3 − 0.5 = _____

2. $\frac{3}{4}$
       $-\frac{1}{4}$
       ‾‾‾‾

3. What is the perimeter of this rectangle?

```
      4 cm
┌──────────┐
│          │ 1 cm
└──────────┘
```

_____

4. What is the area of the rectangle in problem 3?

_____

5. Minnie found 16 pennies, 4 nickels, 3 dimes, 6 quarters, and 2 one-dollar bills in her purse. How much money does she have?

_____

EMC 754 • © Evan-Moor Corp.

Wednesday 8

1. 8 × 3 = _____

2.   34
     x 2

3. What is a quotient?

_____

_____

_____

4. What is the perimeter of this triangle?

_____

4 in.

5. Mrs. Watson has a jar of beads. There are 50 red beads, 50 blue beads, and 50 green beads. If a student sticks his or her hand in the jar and pulls out a bead, what is the probability that it will be blue?

_____

How would the probability change if Mrs. Watson added 50 red beads?

_____

Thursday 8

1. 95 ÷ 5 = _____

2. 6)240

3. What are the next five figures in this pattern?

 ●▼◆●▼I●▼◆●▼I __ __ __ __ __

4. What are the common factors of 10 and 5?

_____

5. Karl piled twelve 1" cubes in three layers on top of a square made with four 1" cubes. What shape is the structure that Karl made?

_____

Friday ⬡ 8

Determine the volume of each box.
What conclusion can you draw about the boxes?

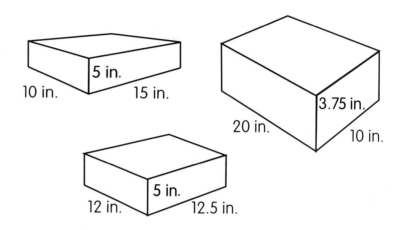

Daily Progress Record ⬡ 8

How many did you get correct each day? Color the squares.

	Monday	Tuesday	Wednesday	Thursday	Friday
5					
4					
3					
2					
1					

EMC 754 • © Evan-Moor Corp.

1. 6.5 + 4.7 = _____

2.   684
   + 539

3. How do you know if a number is divisible by 5?

_____

_____

_____

4. Round 4,379,821 to the nearest hundred.

_____

5. Polly the parrot has learned to say, "Polly wants a cracker." If she repeats the phrase every five minutes for two hours and is given a cracker each time she asks for one, how many crackers will she eat?

_____

1. 32.04 − 10.42 = _____

2.   6,394
   − 2,918

3. Identify the fractions represented by A and B.

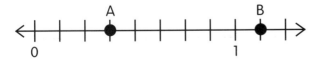

4. What is 50% of 84?

_____

5. Farmer McDonald is building a fence. He will place posts six feet apart and stretch the wire fencing between the posts. If his pasture is thirty-six feet long and twelve feet across, how many posts will he need?

_____

Wednesday ⟨9⟩

1. 7 x 8 = _____

2. 9.1
      x 4
      ─────

3. 43 + 129 – _____ = 101

4. Which of these is four and six tenths?

a. 4.06   c. 4.6

b. 46   d. 4 & 6 & 10

5. Owen was stacking popcorn balls on a table. He put sixteen balls on the table. He added three more layers. Each layer had four fewer balls than the previous layer. How many popcorn balls in all did Owen put on the table?

_____

Thursday ⟨9⟩

1. 92 ÷ 2 = _____

2. 5⟌640

3. If a rectangle measures 8 inches by 23 inches, what is its area?

_____

4. What is the mode of this data?

2, 4, 5, 3, 2, 7, 4, 2, 8, 1, 5

_____

5. In the election 46% of the class voted for Celina. If there are 50 members in the class, how many votes did Celina receive?

_____

EMC 754 • © Evan-Moor Corp.

Friday 9

Graph the following ordered pairs:

(6, 5) (5, 1) (2, 1) (3, 5)

Draw a line to connect the points. What shape have you created?

Name the point that is 5 points below and 6 points to the left of (2, 1).

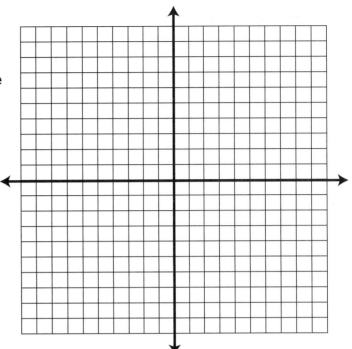

Daily Math Practice

Daily Progress Record 9

How many did you get correct each day? Color the squares.

	Monday	Tuesday	Wednesday	Thursday	Friday
5					
4					
3					
2					
1					

1. $3\frac{1}{4} + 2\frac{3}{4} =$ _____

2.   985
       + 785

3. What is the least common multiple (LCM) of 6 and 10?

_____

4. Write $\frac{1}{2}$ as a percent.

_____

5. Draw and label a Venn diagram for the intersection of these sets.

A = 2, 4, 6, 8, 10
B = 5, 10, 20, 30, 40

1. $6\frac{3}{4} - 3\frac{1}{4} =$ _____

2.   873
       − 495

3. Simplify this expression.

$(6 \times 2) - 4$

_____

4. What is the probability of spinning a 3?

_____

5. What is the team's average score?
Game 1–69
Game 2–48
Game 3–57
Game 4–70
Game 5–66

_____

   EMC 754 • © Evan-Moor Corp.

1. $\frac{1}{2} \times 5 =$ _____

2. 35.4
   x 2.1

3. Write this number in standard form.

   ten thousand forty

   _____

4. Complete this table. Tell how you determined
   the missing numbers.

Input	Output
2	4
3	9
4	16
5	
6	
7	

   _____

   _____

   _____

   _____

5. If Rhoda buys six 12-packs of fruit snacks for
   $14.40, how much does each fruit snack cost?

   _____

1. 38)7.6

2. 64)1,600

3. Write the next two numbers in this sequence.

   80, 40, 20, _____, _____

4. What is the area of this figure?

   _____

5. Roger is planning a picnic. He will invite two
   times as many boys as girls. If he invites
   18 people, how many boys and how many
   girls will get invitations?

   _____

Boris is painting boxes that are stacked one on top of the other. He paints only the sides (not the top or the bottom) of each box. He will, however, paint the top of the box at the very top of the stack.

How many faces does he paint in a stack of

three boxes? _____

five boxes? _____

eleven boxes? _____

Create a function table to show the number of boxes and the faces painted. What is the rule for the table?

Daily Math Practice

Daily Progress Record ⟨10⟩

How many did you get correct each day? Color the squares.

	Monday	Tuesday	Wednesday	Thursday	Friday
5					
4					
3					
2					
1					

EMC 754 • © Evan-Moor Corp.

1. 6.5 + 8.3 = _____

2.   8,643
       + 7,968

3. If the product of two numbers is 21 and the sum is 10, what are the two numbers?

_____

4. If two angles of a triangle each measure 45 degrees, what is the third angle?

_____

5. Cam collected twenty-five soda cans. Five of the cans are root beer cans. What fraction of the collected cans are root beer? Express the fraction as a percent.

_____

---

1. 9.4 − 3.7 = _____

2.   652
       − 288

3. Fill in the correct symbol.

$< = >$

⁻4 ◯ ⁻6

4. What place value does the 8 have in 1,386,672?

_____

5. Trevor is $8\frac{1}{2}$ inches shorter than his dad. If his dad is six feet tall, how tall is Trevor?

_____

1. $\frac{1}{3} \times \frac{1}{4} =$ _____

2.   280
        x 16

3. How many faces does a rectangular prism have?

_____

4. Write this number in standard form.

one hundred sixteen and six tenths

_____

5. Lena and Antonio baby-sat three children for five hours. If they are paid $2.50 per hour for each child, how much did they earn?

_____

1. $4.9 \div 7 =$ _____

2. 15)1,230

3. Identify the fractions represented by A and B.

_____

4. Write the next two numbers in this pattern.

1, 1, 4, 4, 7, 7, _____, _____

5. Patrice went to two stores and compared the price of gummi worms. At the Save-More Market, gummi worms are $3.95 per pound. At the Buy-Here Warehouse, the price is two pounds for $6.50. Which store has the better buy? Explain your answer.

_____

_____

_____

Friday ⟨11⟩

Graph the attendance for each game.

8/10 = 42,600
8/11 = 44,000
8/12 = 40,800
8/13 = 45,400
8/14 = 45,800

What was the total attendance for all playoff games combined? (Give your answer to the nearest thousand.)

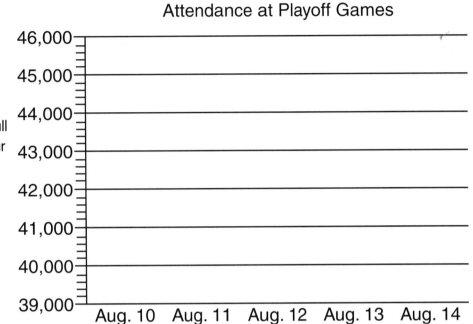

Attendance at Playoff Games

Daily Math Practice

Daily Progress Record ⟨11⟩

How many did you get correct each day? Color the squares.

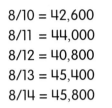

	Monday	Tuesday	Wednesday	Thursday	Friday
5					
4					
3					
2					
1					

© Evan-Moor Corp.

1. $\frac{3}{4} + \frac{1}{3} =$ _____

2.   789
        + 321

3. Which of these figures are congruent?

A   B   C   D   E

_____

4. Write 6,352.8 in word form.

_____

_____

5. Marek is saving for a new computer game. The game will cost $39.99. He has saved $27. How much more does he need?

_____

1. $87.62 - 48.95 =$ _____

2. 6
       $- 2\frac{1}{2}$

3. What is the volume of this rectangular prism?

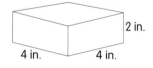

2 in.
4 in.   4 in.

_____

4. What is the greatest common factor (GCF) of 6 and 9?

_____

5. The temperature on a cold December morning fell from 37° to ⁻4°. How many degrees did the temperature fall?

_____

EMC 754 • © Evan-Moor Corp.

Wednesday ⟨12⟩

1. 757 × 30 = _____

2.   3.9
     × 2.3

3. What is 13 hours after 12:00 midnight?

_____

4. What are the next three numbers in this pattern?

2, 5, 3, 5, 4, 5, _____, _____, _____

5. Mrs. Diaz wants new carpet for her living room. How many square yards will she need?

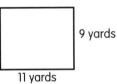

9 yards

11 yards

_____

If the carpet costs $15.99 a square yard, how much will it cost?

_____

Thursday ⟨12⟩

1. $\frac{1}{4} \div \frac{1}{2}$ = _____

2. 30)15.90

3. 10% of 20 = _____

4. Draw the shape of this ice-cream cone wrapper when it is slit from the edge to the center point and flattened out.

5. Jana and Anton walk home from school on Monday, Wednesday, and Friday. Their mother picks them up on Thursday and they ride the bus on Tuesday. What fraction of the time do they walk home?

_____

ride the bus? _____

Friday ⟨12⟩

The Lowe family always orders a two-topping pizza. How many different combinations do they have to choose from if there are five toppings on the menu?

Show your work here.

Write your answer here.

Daily Progress Record ⟨12⟩

How many did you get correct each day? Color the squares.

	Monday	Tuesday	Wednesday	Thursday	Friday
5					
4					
3					
2					
1					

EMC 754 • © Evan-Moor Corp.

1. 3.8 × 2.5 = _____

2. 4,320
       +   84

3. What solid is formed by folding this pattern?

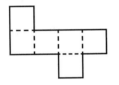

_____

4. Circle the prime numbers.

   2   92   59   6   5   12

5. A motorcyclist used 3.21 liters of gasoline to travel from Greenfield to Milltown. The next day he traveled from Milltown to New Haven, using another 1.95 liters of gasoline. About how much gas did he use on the two trips?

○ about 4 liters   ○ about 5 liters

○ about 3 liters   ○ about 6 liters

---

1. 324 − 192 = _____

2. $\frac{3}{4}$
       $-\frac{1}{8}$

3. Write this number in standard notation.

   forty-five thousand three hundred sixty-six

   _____

4. Match the parts of the circle to the correct labels.

diameter _____

center _____

radius _____

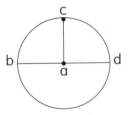

5. During the candy sale, the three students in Matt's group raised $732.53. Bob sold $232.46 worth of candy and Cathy sold $189.21. How much did Matt sell?

_____

Wednesday ⟨13⟩

1. 64 x 18 = _____

2. $1\frac{1}{2}$
   $\times\ 3$

3. Simplify this expression.

   $(16 - 8) + 5$

   _____

4. Write the next three numbers in this pattern.

   2, 8, 32, _____, _____, _____

5. Ms. Black has one begonia plant. If she buys two begonia plants each year for every one she has, how many will she have in four years?

   _____

Thursday ⟨13⟩

1. $\frac{3}{5} \div \frac{3}{2} =$ _____

2. $48\overline{)1,632}$

3. Reduce this fraction to lowest terms.

   $\frac{6}{8}$

   _____

4. What is the range of this data?

   17, 23, 5, 13, 12

   _____

5. A class donates $1.50 per student to the park project. If the total donation is $52.50, how many students are there?

   _____

EMC 754 • © Evan-Moor Corp.

Mr. Giles gave four tests during the semester. Each test was worth 100 points. On the first test, Carey got a score of 85. On the second test, he scored 92. He earned 70 points on the third test. On the last test, he received 96 points. Complete this line graph to show Carey's test scores.

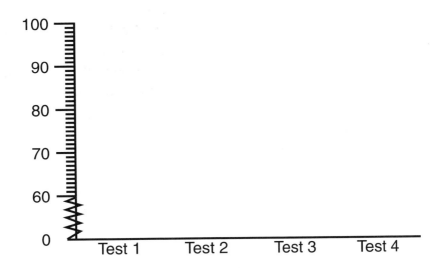

How many did you get correct each day? Color the squares.

	Monday	Tuesday	Wednesday	Thursday	Friday
5					
4					
3					
2					
1					

Monday ⟨14⟩

1. 18 + 17 + 42 = _____

2. $\dfrac{8}{9}$
   $+ \dfrac{4}{12}$
   _____

3. Round the number 894,754,390 to the nearest million.

   _____

4. What shape is the base of a cube?

   _____

5. This chart shows Yvonne's savings account balance. If she continues to save at this rate, how much money will she have at the end of 8 weeks?

Week	Account Balance
1	$2.00
2	$3.50
3	$5.00

   _____

Tuesday ⟨14⟩

1. $6\frac{1}{2} - 4 =$ _____

2.   10,000
   −   47
   _____

3. Give one good reason why 2,800 is <u>not</u> a good estimate for 702 x 43.

   _____

   _____

   _____

4. Find the LCM of 3, 7, and 6.

   _____

5. Four students (Misu, Tala, Kane, and Marie) compared their math scores: 99, 92, 86, and 100. Use these clues to match the students with their scores.

   Clues:
   1. Misu scored higher than Kane and lower than Marie.
   2. Tala's score was higher than Kane's and lower than Misu's.

   _____

   _____

EMC 754 • © Evan-Moor Corp.

1. 0.503 x 0.27 = _____

2. $\frac{3}{5}$

  x $\frac{3}{10}$

3. What is the surface area of a 3" cube?

_____

4. 9 : 3 :: 49 : _____

5. Steve exercises by rollerblading. He skates 4 kilometers on Mondays, 5 kilometers on Thursdays, 8 kilometers on Saturdays, and 10 kilometers on Sundays. If he clocked 17 kilometers for the week, on which days did he skate?

_____

1. $\frac{3}{4} \div \frac{2}{3}$ = _____

2. 6$\overline{)44.10}$

3. If the average of these four numbers is 21, find the missing number.

  12 18 28 _____

4. Define a square.

_____

_____

_____

5. Caramel apples cost $2. There is a 50¢ charge for nuts or chips. Tori wants a caramel apple with nuts. Chelsea wants both nuts and chips on her apple. Max wants his caramel apple plain. How much will the three apples cost?

_____

Friday 14

The frozen yogurt shop sells cones in five different sizes. Read this chart and determine the best buy.

Yogurt Cones		
Size		Price
Baby Cup	6 ounces	$1.25
Small	8 ounces	$2.00
Regular	12 ounces	$3.00
Large	16 ounces	$4.00
Giant	24 ounces	$5.50

Daily Math Practice

Daily Progress Record 14

How many did you get correct each day? Color the squares.

	Monday	Tuesday	Wednesday	Thursday	Friday
5					
4					
3					
2					
1					

EMC 754 • © Evan-Moor Corp.

1. 2,804 + 9,782 = _____

2. 18,706
   − 3,897

3. What is the largest number you can make with these digits?

   8 2 9 0

   _____

4. If six equilateral triangles are placed side by side so that only two sides of each triangle touch one of the other triangles, what shape is formed?

   _____

5. The traffic officer clocked the cars at 45 mph, 37 mph, 34 mph, and 40 mph. What is the average speed?

   _____

1. $3\frac{1}{2} - 2\frac{1}{4} =$ _____

2. 97,000
   − 3,529

3. List all the factors of 28.

   _____

4. Name the first three prime numbers.

   _____

5. Scotty and his dad are repairing the railing along the side of the deck. They put up eight supports with 4 feet between each one. If the first support is at one corner of the deck and the eighth support is at the other corner, how long is the side?

   _____

Wednesday ⟨15⟩

1. 189.45 x 81.6 = _____

2. $\frac{3}{4}$
    x $\frac{1}{8}$
    _____

3. How many ounces are in 4 pounds?

_____

4. Which is larger, 0.06 or 0.018?

_____

5. An inchworm crawling up a branch climbs 100 centimeters the first hour, 90 centimeters the second hour, and 80 centimeters the third hour. How many centimeters will it travel after 5 hours?

_____

Thursday ⟨15⟩

1. 3.5 ÷ 7 = _____

2. 75⟌98,605

3. If you have a 3-cup container and a 5-cup container, how can you measure exactly 1 cup?

_____

_____

4. Define a circle.

_____

_____

_____

5. There was 1 marble in the first sack, 3 marbles in the second sack, 6 marbles in the third sack, and 10 marbles in the fourth sack. How many marbles would be in the fifth sack?

_____

EMC 754 • © Evan-Moor Corp.

Friday ⟨15⟩

Create a picture graph to represent the following information. Be sure to include a key to explain the graph symbol used.

Books Read During "I Love to Read" Week
mysteries = 150
biographies = 65
adventure stories = 175
science fiction = 90
realistic fiction = 165

Daily Math Practice

Daily Progress Record ⟨15⟩

How many did you get correct each day? Color the squares.

	Monday	Tuesday	Wednesday	Thursday	Friday
5					
4					
3					
2					
1					

Monday 〈16〉

1. 0.05 + 1.37 = _____

2. 763,199
   +   3,672

3. The highest temperature on Monday was 30°C. If the average high temperature for the week was 45°C, what statement can you make about Monday's temperature?

_____

4. What is the value of a in this equation?

$$3 \times a = 24$$

_____

5. Max's purchase at the clothing store totaled $72.27. If he paid with four $20 bills, what change did he receive? Tell one way that the clerk might have made that amount.

_____

_____

_____

Tuesday 〈16〉

1. 97,203 − 59,868 = _____

2.   3.69
   − 0.01

3. Find the perimeter and the area of this figure.

4. Which of these fractions is greater?

$\frac{5}{6}$ $\frac{7}{8}$

_____

5. Clovertown students attend school five days a week for thirty-six weeks. Each school day is six hours long. How many hours do students spend in school each year?

_____

_____

EMC 754 • © Evan-Moor Corp.

Wednesday ⟨16⟩

1. $9.6 \times 0.37 =$ _____

2. $\dfrac{1}{2}$
   $\times \dfrac{6}{7}$

3. Two intersecting lines are parallel.

   true   false

4. Which digit is in the tenths place?

   145.6

   _____

5. Elsa bought a pizza for dinner. On the way home she ate $\frac{1}{8}$ of the pizza. Her brother ate $\frac{1}{4}$ of the pizza while he was setting the table. How much pizza was left for dinner?

   _____

Thursday ⟨16⟩

1. $1\frac{1}{2} \div \frac{3}{4} =$ _____

2. $12\overline{)7.32}$

3. Draw an obtuse angle.

4. Which of these numbers is forty-five thousand three hundred sixty-six?

   ○ 4,530,066   ○ 4,536

   ○ 45,366   ○ 453,066

5. In one class there are 15 boys and 12 girls. On Wednesday all the girls were present and $\frac{1}{5}$ of the boys were absent. How many students were in the class?

   _____

Friday ⟨16⟩

Todd is moving sand from his driveway to the backyard. The wheelbarrow weighs 30 kilograms when it is full of sand. When it is empty, it weighs 12 kilograms. How much sand did Todd move if he filled and emptied the wheelbarrow five times?

Show your work here.

Write your answer here.

Daily Progress Record ⟨16⟩

How many did you get correct each day? Color the squares.

	Monday	Tuesday	Wednesday	Thursday	Friday
5					
4					
3					
2					
1					

EMC 754 • © Evan-Moor Corp.

1. $5\frac{1}{4} + 2\frac{1}{4} =$ _____

2.
```
   5,782
   3,491
+     69
```

3. Round 369.2284 to the nearest thousandth.

_____

4. What is a perimeter?

_____

_____

_____

5. Mirette wants to plant bulbs in patterned rows in her garden. Each row will have 12 plants alternating in this pattern: red tulip, yellow tulip, yellow tulip, white tulip. If she plants 8 rows, how many bulbs of each color will she need?

_____

1. 98,234 – 998 = _____

2.
$$9\frac{1}{5}$$
$$-\ \frac{3}{5}$$
_____

3. How many fourths are there in six-eighths?

_____

4. Write the next three numbers in this pattern.

3   6   4   8   6   12 ____ ____ ____

5. Scott uses three 14-gallon tanks of gas a month. What is the average number of gallons he uses daily in a 30-day month? (Give your answer to the nearest half gallon.)

_____

Wednesday ⟨17⟩

1. 902 x 2.08 = _____

2. 8.34
    x 0.5

3. Order these numbers from smallest to largest.

   971   91.7   17.9   197   0.791   7.19

   _____

4. A square is a rectangle.

   true   false

5. Tweety eats one ounce of birdseed each day. About how many weeks will a five-pound bag of birdseed last?

   _____

Thursday ⟨17⟩

1. $\frac{3}{4} \div \frac{1}{9} =$ _____

2. $22\overline{)8,030}$

3. What is 7^2?

   _____

4. Draw a right angle.

5. Members of the band are required to practice twenty-five minutes every night. About how many hours does a band member practice weekly?

   _____

EMC 754 • © Evan-Moor Corp.

Friday 〈17〉

Marc built a fence around his henhouse. He used one post every eight feet and one roll of chicken wire.

How many posts did he use?_____

How long was the roll of chicken wire?_____

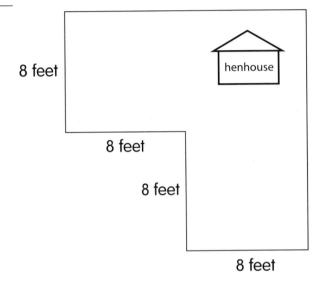

Daily Math Practice

Daily Progress Record 〈17〉

How many did you get correct each day? Color the squares.

	Monday	Tuesday	Wednesday	Thursday	Friday
5					
4					
3					
2					
1					

1. 783 + 348 + 106 = _____

2. $149.08
       + 327.14
       ⎯⎯⎯⎯⎯⎯

3. If each triangle is equilateral, what is the outer perimeter of this shape?

 3 in.

_____

4. 8^3 = _____

5. The stadium capacity allows for players, radio and newspaper reporters, and stadium workers in addition to spectators. How many of these people could be at a game?

Victory Stadium	
Stadium capacity	42,500
General admission seating	31,750
Reserved seating	10,475

_____

1. 8,241 − 3,687 = _____

2. $29.00
       −   4.99
       ⎯⎯⎯⎯⎯⎯

3. Give the value of z.

$$4 \times 2 - z = 7$$

_____

4. About how much rain fell over these three days?

Day	Amount (in inches)
Sunday	1.9
Tuesday	3.3
Friday	0.9

◯ about 4 inches   ◯ about 10 inches

◯ about 6 inches

5. On Saturday, Mike did one hundred twenty-six sit-ups in six minutes. How many sit-ups is that per minute?

_____

EMC 754 • © Evan-Moor Corp.

1. 249 x 281 = _____

2. 2.5
 x 0.06

3. Draw a picture to show $\frac{4}{3}$.

4. Which of these is a common multiple of 6 and 8?

15   68   24   90   9

_____

5. A one-way trolley ticket to Old Town costs $1.50. How much will it cost for Diego and three friends to ride to Old Town and home again?

_____

1. $\frac{1}{2} \div \frac{1}{7}$ = _____

2. 15)123,045

3. What is the average (mean) of this data?

4, 12, 23, 11, 5

_____

4. If the product of two numbers is 56 and the sum is 15, what are the two numbers?

_____

5. Jenna is going to paint one wall of her bedroom gray. She needs a gallon of paint. A gallon of paint costs $17.00 and one quart of paint costs $4.39. Which is the better buy?

_____

Use the digits 1 through 9 to complete these number sentences. Use each digit only once.

_____ + _____ = 10

_____ + _____ = _____

_____ + _____ = 12

_____ + _____ = 7

Daily Math Practice

Daily Progress Record ⟨18⟩

How many did you get correct each day? Color the squares.

	Monday	Tuesday	Wednesday	Thursday	Friday
5					▓
4					
3					
2					
1					

EMC 754 • © Evan-Moor Corp.

1. 2.37 + 82.9 = _____

2.   10,948
       – 6,819

3. List all the factors of 24.

_____

4. Add **two** operational signs to make the equation true.

2   4   6   1   3 = 88

5. Bill cut open and flattened this box for recycling. What shape was the box before it was flattened?

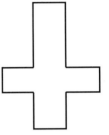

_____

---

1. $\frac{1}{5} + \frac{1}{2} =$ _____

2.   7.20
       – 0.9

3. How many ounces are in 3 pounds?

_____

4. Write 4,801 in word form.

_____

5. It takes one hour for Alice to walk to her grandmother's house. She walked ten minutes and then stopped for a soda. After walking another fifteen minutes, she stopped for an ice-cream cone. In another fifteen minutes, she stopped to visit with Mrs. Smith. What fraction of the trip had Alice completed when she stopped to visit with Mrs. Smith?

_____

1. 80,192 x 0 + 34 = _____

2. $\frac{1}{8}$
   $+ \frac{3}{5}$
   _____

3. Reduce $\frac{36}{42}$ to its lowest form.

_____

4. Circle the first number that is incorrect in this work:

$$\begin{array}{r} 461,592 \\ \times \quad\quad 308 \\ \hline 3592736 \\ \underline{13947760\quad} \\ 142,070,336 \end{array}$$

5. Justine can make one place mat out of $\frac{1}{2}$ yard of material. If she has 5 feet of material, how many place mats can she make?

_____

1. 5.34 ÷ 4 = _____

2.   1,000
   $\times$ 357
   _____

3. Find the LCM of 7 and 6.

_____

4. What comes next?

8 4 10 6 12 8 _____

5. Six hundred people came to the band concert that was held on the school's athletic field. Half of the people sat in the bleachers. One-third of the people sat in chairs on the track. The rest of the people sat on the grass.

How many sat on the grass?_____

in chairs? _____

in the bleachers?_____

EMC 754 • © Evan-Moor Corp.

Friday 〈19〉

Brett, May, James, and Elisa were each given a present. Use the clues and the grid to decide which present each child received.

Clue 1: James did not get the present with the green ribbon.
Clue 2: May's present had a bow the same color as her bunny's nose.
Clue 3: Only Brett's ribbon color begins with the same letter as his name.

	Blue	Green	Pink	White
James				
May				
Brett				
Elisa				

Daily Math Practice

Daily Progress Record 〈19〉

How many did you get correct each day? Color the squares.

	Monday	Tuesday	Wednesday	Thursday	Friday
5					
4					
3					
2					
1					

1. What is the square of 12? _____

2. $\begin{array}{r} 9.5 \\ \times\,4.2 \\ \hline \end{array}$

3. Write 75.9 in word form.

   _____

4. Find the median of this data.

   4, 7, 9, 10, 5, 12, 6

   _____

5. A recipe calls for three cups of cheese to make nachos for six people. How much cheese is needed to make nachos for two dozen people?

   _____

1. $4 \div 5 =$ _____

2. $\begin{array}{r} 2 \\ +\,3 \\ \hline \end{array}$

3. What comes next in this pattern?

   2 12 32 62 102 _____

4. 3 : 15 :: 60 : _____

5. A baby weighed eight pounds and three ounces at birth. If the baby weighed twelve pounds and five ounces at three months of age, how much weight did the baby gain?

   _____

1. 109 x 37 = _____

2. $2\frac{3}{4}$
$+ 4\frac{1}{6}$

3. What is 50% of 20?

_____

4. What is the volume of this cube?

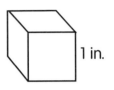

1 in.

_____

5. The fruit in the bowl is $\frac{1}{2}$ apples and $\frac{1}{3}$ bananas. The rest of the fruit is oranges. What fraction of the fruit is oranges?

_____

1. 16 x 2.6 = _____

2. $2\frac{2}{5}$
$+ 3\frac{3}{4}$

3. Fill in the correct symbol.

< = >

35.6  3.65

4. If $a = 4$ and $b = 2$, then $3a + 3b$ equals

_____.

5. The school choir members have collected 6,000 aluminum cans. If the recycling center pays $2 for 500 cans, how much money will the choir earn?

_____

Friday ⟨20⟩

Plot these points on the grid. Then connect the points.

(6, 4) (⁻2, 4) (6, ⁻4) (⁻2, ⁻4)

Determine the center point of the figure you created. Write its coordinates.

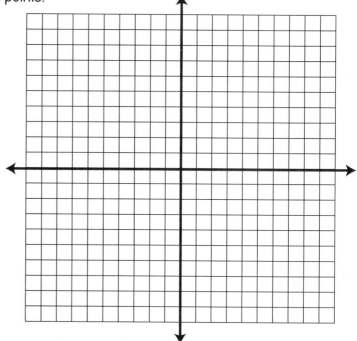

Daily Progress Record ⟨20⟩

How many did you get correct each day? Color the squares.

	Monday	Tuesday	Wednesday	Thursday	Friday
5					
4					
3					
2					
1					

EMC 754 • © Evan-Moor Corp.

1. $666 \div 9 =$ _____

2. $\begin{array}{r} 346 \\ \times\ 648 \\ \hline \end{array}$

3. How many minutes are in 3 hours and 25 minutes?

_____

4. Explain this pattern.

322   32.2   3.22   0.322

_____

_____

_____

5. Chet's watch is guaranteed for 90 days. If it stops working six weeks after he bought it, is it still under warranty?

_____

---

1. $\frac{1}{2} \div \frac{1}{2} =$ _____

2. $\begin{array}{r} 6.21 \\ \times\ \ \ 35 \\ \hline \end{array}$

3. $a \times 0 =$ _____

4. Round 92,187 to the nearest hundred.

_____

5. Cecily is swinging. The swing goes back and forth twice every five seconds. How many seconds does it take her to go back and forth one hundred times?

_____

About how many minutes is that?

_____

Wednesday ⟨**21**⟩

1. $7.6 + 0.18 =$ _____

2. $^-35 - 4 =$ _____

3. Estimate 197×24. Explain how you made your estimation.

   _____

   _____

   _____

4. $2^3 =$ _____

5. Toshi has six coins that total 91 cents. What are the coins?

   _____

   _____

Thursday ⟨**21**⟩

1. $897,412 + 34,879 =$ _____

2. $\begin{array}{r} 497,002 \\ -\ \underline{36,284} \end{array}$

3. Write 57.3 in word form.

   _____

4. List all the factors of 16.

   _____

5. Amy has 80 photos for her scrapbook. If she can fit 4 photos on each page of the 15 pages she has, how many more pages does she need to buy?

   _____

EMC 754 • © Evan-Moor Corp.

Friday 21

The soccer team scored 100 goals during the spring season. Darin scored 25 goals. Martin scored 10 goals. Sue Ellen scored 15 goals. Lynda scored 50 goals. Make a circle graph to show this information. Title the graph.

What fraction did Lynda score? _____

What fraction did Darin score? _____

Daily Math Practice

Daily Progress Record 〈21〉

How many did you get correct each day? Color the squares.

	Monday	Tuesday	Wednesday	Thursday	Friday
5					
4					
3					
2					
1					

1. 783 + 348 + 106 = _____

2. 7,300
     − 4,082

3. Order these numbers from smallest to largest.

8.00   8.30   0.800   0.83

_____

4. Solve for *x*.

$$2x = 368 - 4$$

_____

5. At the ballgame, Isabelle bought two hot dogs ($2.25 each), two sodas ($1 each), and one bag of peanuts ($1.50). If she gave the cashier a ten-dollar bill, how much did she get back?

_____

---

1. 2(9 × 3) = _____

2. $4.85
     − 2.56

3. It is 10 degrees outside, and the temperature is due to drop 16 degrees. What will be the temperature then?

_____

4. Complete the drawing so that it is symmetrical.

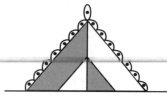

5. Jorge is thirty years younger than his mom. His mom is two years older than Jorge's dad. If Jorge's dad is thirty-nine, how old is Jorge?

_____

     EMC 754 • © Evan-Moor Corp.

1. $\frac{4}{7} + \frac{1}{2} =$ _____

2. $\begin{array}{r} \frac{3}{4} \\ \times\ \frac{4}{5} \\ \hline \end{array}$

3. What is 20% of 10?

_____

4. What place value does the 4 have in 2.6741?

_____

5. Maisie is writing a report about kangaroos. The report must be two full pages. If there are twenty lines on each page and each line has about 20 words, about how many words long does Maisie's report need to be?

_____

1. $\frac{3}{8} + 1\frac{3}{8} =$ _____

2. $\begin{array}{r} 8{,}582 \\ -\ 3{,}909 \\ \hline \end{array}$

3. Evaluate the expression $2a + 4a + a$, if $a = 6$.

_____

4. How many feet are in 7 yards?

_____

How many inches?

_____

5. In how many different ways can three candles be arranged on the table if they are in a straight line horizontally?

_____

Friday ⟨22⟩

Magic Square

Use the numbers 4, 8, 12, 16, 20, 24, 28, 32, and 36. Write one number in each square. The sums of all the rows, columns, and diagonals should be 60.

Daily Progress Record ⟨22⟩

How many did you get correct each day? Color the squares.

	Monday	Tuesday	Wednesday	Thursday	Friday
5					
4					
3					
2					
1					

     EMC 754 • © Evan-Moor Corp.

1. 13 x 39 = _____

2. $\frac{5}{8}$

  + $\frac{3}{4}$

_____

3. What value of x makes this equation true?

49 – x = 35

_____

4. Name this figure.

_____

5. Twelve students have bikes. Half of the bikes are black and one-sixth of the bikes are silver. The rest of the bikes are other colors.

How many bikes are black? _____

silver? _____

other colors? _____

1. 1.4 ÷ 7 = _____

2.   126
      – 99

3. Write this number in standard form.

six thousand and one hundredth

_____

4. Round 9.098 to the nearest tenth.

_____

5. It takes Omar four minutes to eat eight carrot sticks. How long does it take him to eat one?

_____

1. $392.87 - 100.99 =$ _____

2.
$$\frac{1}{8}$$
$$\frac{2}{3}$$
$$+ \frac{1}{6}$$

3. Rewrite $3\frac{27}{100}$ as a decimal.

_____

4. What are the common factors of 4 and 10?

_____

5. The staff at the pretzel shop bakes eight trays of twelve pretzels each every hour. If the staff works eight hours a day, how many pretzels do they bake a day?

_____

1. $9.9 \div 33 =$ _____

2.
$$900$$
$$\times 146$$

3. $\frac{1}{4}$ of a dozen eggs = _____

4. Find the perimeter of this figure.

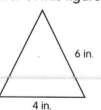

6 in.

4 in.

_____

5. Mr. Nutty had 100 jars of peanut butter. He sold one dozen jars each day last week. How many jars does he have left?

_____

EMC 754 • © Evan-Moor Corp.

Friday ⟨23⟩

Use the map below to solve this problem.

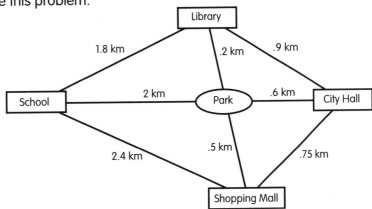

Tabitha walked from school to the library and then to the park.

Jennie ran from the park to the shopping mall and then to City Hall.

From school, Alexis rode her bike to the park, then on to the library, and finally back to school.

Barb walked the entire perimeter of the area shown on the map.

What is the total distance traveled by all the girls?

Daily Math Practice

Daily Progress Record ⟨23⟩

How many did you get correct each day? Color the squares.

	Monday	Tuesday	Wednesday	Thursday	Friday
5					
4					
3					
2					
1					

1. $9.6 \div 20 =$ _____

2. $\begin{array}{r} ^-10 \\ + 23 \\ \hline \end{array}$

3. Add a sign.

3 6 4 2 0 $= 7{,}280$

4. Write about how you would compute this problem.

$432 - 49$

_____

_____

_____

5. The number is between 20 and 40. It is an odd number. Its digits add up to 8. The larger digit minus the other digit is 2. What is the number?

_____

1. $7^2 =$ _____

2. $\frac{1}{2} \div \frac{6}{7} =$ _____

3. What is the mode of this data?

8, 4, 12, 23, 11, 5, 38, 15, 8, 27, 3

_____

4. Find the area of this figure.

6 cm   4 cm

_____

5. Alf's family will drive to his grandmother's house. While they are on the road, it costs $56 a day for gas, $47 a day for food, and $60 a night for lodging. It will take them three days and two nights to get there. How much will it cost for the round trip?

_____

EMC 754 • © Evan-Moor Corp.

Wednesday ⟨24⟩

1. ⁻12 + 4 = _____

2.   0.37
     x 1.08

3. What are the next two numbers in this pattern?

   88 44 64 32 52 _____ _____

4. What value of b makes this a true number sentence?

   $$9b + 5 = 41$$

   _____

5. Willem bought a jacket on sale. The price was 40% off the original price of $60. How much did he pay?

   _____

Thursday ⟨24⟩

1. 3^3 = _____

2. $\frac{1}{10}$
     $+ 1\frac{1}{2}$

3. A balance scale is perfectly balanced with two blocks on one side and ten weights on the other. If each weight equals 2.0 grams, how much does one block weigh?

   _____

4. What is the LCM of 2, 4, and 5?

   _____

5. Sally answered 90% of the math test questions and 80% of the history test questions correctly. If each test had 50 questions, how many questions in all did she answer correctly?

   _____

Friday ⟨24⟩

When Dean counts his beanbag animals, he has three times as many mammals as birds and reptiles together. He has twice as many reptiles as birds. He has a total of 48 animals. How many birds, reptiles, and mammals does he have?

Show your work here.

Write your answer here.

Daily Progress Record ⟨24⟩

How many did you get correct each day? Color the squares.

	Monday	Tuesday	Wednesday	Thursday	Friday
5					
4					
3					
2					
1					

EMC 754 • © Evan-Moor Corp.

1. $10^3 =$ _____

2. $2^4 =$ _____

3. Find the GCF of 25 and 41.

_____

4. Which of these weighs the most?

   ○ 0.001 kilogram   ○ 10 grams

5. If Paul saves $3 every week for twelve weeks and then buys a CD for $15, how much money will he have left?

_____

1. $^-20 + 15 =$ _____

2. $^-2 + {}^-5 =$ _____

3. Write four numbers that are less than 5 and greater than 3.

_____

4. Write the next two numbers in this pattern.

   72 86 75 89 80 _____ _____

5. Anneke's science class measured ten inches of rainfall during the month of May. What was the average rainfall per day? (Round your answer to the nearest hundredth.)

_____

Wednesday 〈25〉

1. $\frac{1}{6} \times \frac{4}{5} =$ _____

2. $3\frac{1}{3}$

   $+ 1\frac{1}{4}$
   _____

3. $(9 \times 5) + Z = 48$, if $Z = 3$.

   true   false

4. 80% of a number is 60. What is the number?

   _____

5. Peter grew an average of $\frac{1}{2}$" a month last year. If he was 4' 6" tall at the beginning of the year, how tall was he at the end of the year?

   _____

Daily Math Practice

Thursday 〈25〉

1. $^-3 + 6 =$ _____

2. $^-10 + 3 =$ _____

3. What is 88,855 rounded to the nearest hundred?

   _____

4. List all the factors of 18.

   _____

5. The soccer team played twenty-four games this year. The team won four more games than they lost. How many games did they lose?

   _____

EMC 754 • © Evan-Moor Corp.

Complete this pattern.
What number belongs in the shaded block?

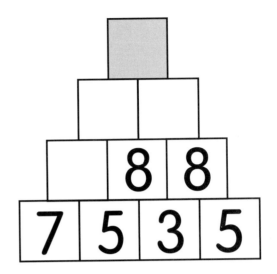

Daily Progress Record ⟨25⟩

How many did you get correct each day? Color the squares.

	Monday	Tuesday	Wednesday	Thursday	Friday
5					
4					
3					
2					
1					

1. (18 + 7) − 10 = _____

2. 8^2 = _____

3. Write 210% as a decimal.

_____

4. Find the area of this figure.

$7\frac{1}{2}$ feet

$3\frac{1}{4}$ feet

_____

5. Every group of three students needs a soccer ball and two cones. If there are thirty students, how many cones do they need?

_____

soccer balls?

_____

1. $\frac{2}{3} + 6\frac{1}{5}$ = _____

2. 60% of 20 = ?

○ 1,200   ○ 12   ○ 120

3. Which two figures are congruent?

A   B   C   D

_____

4. Complete this table.
Multiply by 2.
Add 10.

Input	Output
1	
2	
3	

5. If Jo is supposed to read one-half of a 100-page book for an English assignment and she has finished 38 pages, what percent of the assignment does she have left to do?

_____

1. 89,002 x 386 = _____

2. 25)$38.25

3. If $a - b = 9$ and $a = 36$, give the value of b.

   _____

4. One-half of $3\frac{2}{3}$ = _____

5. The school parking lot had room for thirty cars. If all the spaces except six were filled, what fraction of the parking lot was in use?

   _____

   If Mrs. Johnson parks in one of the empty spaces, how does the fraction change?

   _____

   _____

1. 0.06 x 78 = _____

2.
   $$\begin{array}{r} ^-10 \\ +\ 7 \\ \hline \end{array}$$

3. Estimate 21 x 297.

   _____

4. What are angles that measure less than 90 degrees called?

   _____

5. Seiko has 7 coins (quarters, nickels, and dimes) in her hand. She has the same number of quarters as dimes. Altogether she has $1.10. How many of each coin does she have?

   _____

Friday ⟨26⟩

A **palindrome** is a number that reads the same backwards as it does forward. The number 2332 is an example of a palindrome. Read either way, the number is the same.

To find out if a number can become a palindrome, add the number to its reverse. If it is not yet a palindrome, reverse the sum and add it to the answer. Continue reversing and adding until the answer becomes a palindrome.

Step 1: 57 + 75 = 132
Step 2: 132 + 231 = 363—363 is a two-step palindrome because it goes through two reversals before the answer becomes a palindrome.

Which of these numbers are two-step palindromes?

48   32   91   82   89   76   50   64

Daily Math Practice

Daily Progress Record ⟨26⟩

How many did you get correct each day? Color the squares.

	Monday	Tuesday	Wednesday	Thursday	Friday
5					
4					
3					
2					
1					

  EMC 754 • © Evan-Moor Corp.

1. 8,465 – 2,681 = _____

2. $14,490.08
   +   3,276.15
   _____

3. 88% of $33 = _____

4. If this pattern were made into a solid, what 3-dimensional figure would it be?

_____

5. Fill in the missing signs. (Each shape stands for one sign.) Then write the answer.

   If 31 ◯ 2 ◯ 3 = 186

   13 ☐ 4 ☐ 2 = 7

   128 ▽ 52 ▽ 20 = 200

   Then, 5 ◯ 3 ☐ 12 ▽ 8 = _____

1. 12 ÷ 7 = _____
   (Round your answer to the nearest hundredth.)

2. $\frac{3}{4}$
   $- \frac{1}{3}$
   _____

3. What is the GCF of 3, 7, and 2?

   _____

4. 10^4 is more than 1,000.

   true   false

5. Emma weighed 6 pounds, 9 ounces when she was born. If her weight doubled by the time she was six months old, how much did she weigh then?

   _____

Wednesday (27)

1. 297,450 − 691 = _____

2.   3.02
    x 0.9

3. What comes next?

   1,000   100   10   _____   _____

4. What shape is a soda can?

_____

5. If six more than eight times a number equals thirty, what is the number?

_____

Thursday (27)

1.   8,263
     − 1,097

2. 72)3,672

3. What shape is a brick?

_____

4. List all the multiples of 8 that are less than 100.

_____

5. This chart shows Vic's workout times for the week.

Day	Number of Minutes
Monday	45
Tuesday	50
Wednesday	36
Thursday	70
Friday	49

What was his total time? _____

average (mean) time?   _____

   EMC 754 • © Evan-Moor Corp.

Friday 27

Arrange the numbers 4, 8, 12, 16, 20, 24, 28, 32, and 36 so that the sums of both diagonal lines are 100.

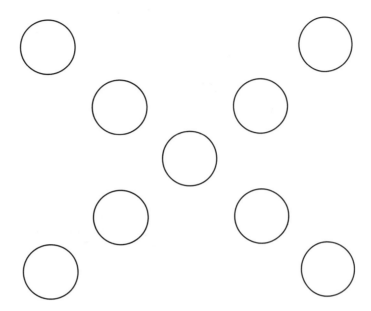

Daily Math Practice

Daily Progress Record 27

How many did you get correct each day? Color the squares.

	Monday	Tuesday	Wednesday	Thursday	Friday
5					
4					
3					
2					
1					

1. 0.034 x 340 = _____

2. Correct the mistakes.   14,687
                            −   9,781
                                5,308

3. Write the factors of 28. Circle the prime factors.

   _____

4. Round 398,669.6 to the nearest whole number.

   _____

5. The sunglasses that Ramon wants to buy are 50% off the original price of $85. If he has to pay 6% tax, what will the glasses cost?

   _____

1. 7.93 − 3.05 = _____

2. 324)5,832

3. Write five million two hundred eighty in standard notation.

   _____

4. Circle the composite numbers.

   92   59   23   47   78   19

5. Dirk has two pet mice. Among other things, he feeds them $\frac{1}{2}$ cup of dry pellets every week. How much dry food will he need for a year?

   _____

EMC 754 • © Evan-Moor Corp.

1. $30 + 10 - 9 =$ _____

2. $\begin{array}{r} {}^{-}17 \\ + \; 11 \\ \hline \end{array}$

3. What are the common factors of 14 and 35?

_____

4. What shape has six sides?

_____

5. Arrange the numbers 2, 4, 6, 8, and 10 so that the sums vertically and horizontally are 18.

1. $1\frac{3}{4} \div 2\frac{1}{3} =$ _____

2. $\begin{array}{r} 0.35 \\ + \; 5.2 \\ \hline \end{array}$

3. What is the perimeter of a triangle whose sides measure 10 cm, 15 cm, and 18 cm?

_____

4. $1^3 =$ _____

5. Sasha flew from San Francisco, California, to Boston, Massachusetts. She took off at 11 A.M. Pacific Time and landed at 7:30 P.M. Eastern Time. If there is a three-hour time difference, how long was Sasha's flight?

_____

Friday ⟨28⟩

Shade in the boxes with the correct factors. When you are done, decode the shaded crisscrossed word.

Factors of 12	5	11	7	7	8	11	9	7	13	9	5	7	10	7	3
Factors of 41	3	2	10	4	11	5	7	6	12	18	9	18	3	2	1
Factors of 60	60	1	5	7	2	12	4	8	3	15	10	9	20	6	30
Factors of 48	3	5	12	9	24	7	4	11	16	11	48	10	1	13	2
Factors of 72	36	12	72	5	4	3	6	7	18	24	8	10	9	2	1
Factors of 19	2	3	19	4	7	11	5	10	5	6	12	9	13	8	8
Factors of 16	8	3	2	7	13	3	10	14	6	15	5	11	9	12	6
Factors of 24	3	2	8	5	7	9	9	13	5	14	11	19	5	10	7

Daily Math Practice

Daily Progress Record ⟨28⟩

How many did you get correct each day? Color the squares.

	Monday	Tuesday	Wednesday	Thursday	Friday
5					
4					
3					
2					
1					

EMC 754 • © Evan-Moor Corp.

1. $3^4 =$ _____

2. $3\frac{1}{2}$
   $4\frac{1}{4}$
   $+ \ \ \frac{3}{5}$
   ‾‾‾‾‾

3. Give the value for x.

   $x \div 5 + 8 = 15$

   _____

4. Write six million four hundred thousand six and six tenths in standard notation.

   _____

5. The pirate captain ordered his men to dig for treasure. Six men dug in equal shifts for a total of three and a half hours. How long was each shift?

   _____

1. $\frac{2}{7} \times 4\frac{1}{2} =$ _____

2. $\ \ \ 0.5$
   $\times\ 0.15$
   ‾‾‾‾‾

3. Patrick left home at 4 P.M. on Sunday. He arrived back home 36 hours later. What day and what time was it?

   _____

4. How many feet are in 15 yards?

   _____

5. Every day, Evy practices piano half as long as she practices gymnastics. She takes half an hour to eat dinner and watches television twice that long. She does homework for an hour more than she practices gymnastics and two hours more than she watches television. How much time does she spend on each activity?

   _____

   _____

   _____

1. $(^-4) + (^-8) =$ _____

2. $\begin{array}{r} 50,097 \\ \times \quad 0.27 \\ \hline \end{array}$

3. What is the GCF of 15, 33, and 54?

   _____

4. What is the measurement of the third angle of a triangle if the first two angles each measure 45 degrees?

   _____

5. Greg wants to divide a $2\frac{1}{2}$-pound block of cheese into four equal pieces. How much will each piece weigh?

   _____

---

1. $^-16 + 8 =$ _____

2. $\begin{array}{r} 7\frac{1}{2} \\ \times \quad \frac{4}{9} \\ \hline \end{array}$

3. Add a sign.

   6   5   8   1   2 = 7,896

4. Write the next two numbers in this pattern.

   44 1 55 2 66 3 77 _____ _____

5. If twenty percent of the students play in the band and the band has forty members, how many students are there?

   _____

EMC 754 • © Evan-Moor Corp.

Below are two views of Cube A.

 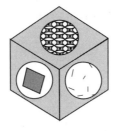

What symbol is opposite this side?

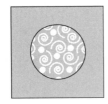

Below are two views of Cube B.

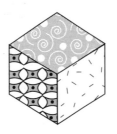 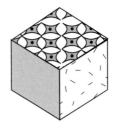

What symbol is opposite this side?

Daily Math Practice

Daily Progress Record 〈29〉

How many did you get correct each day? Color the squares.

	Monday	Tuesday	Wednesday	Thursday	Friday
5					███
4					███
3					███
2					
1					

1. $15^2 =$ _____

2. $7\overline{)2.38}$

3. What is the smallest fraction you can write using the digits 2, 3, and 4?

_____

4. How many cups are in 5 quarts?

_____

5. Rob is $\frac{2}{3}$ of his dad's height. If his dad is 6' 3" tall, how tall is Rob? Give your answer in feet and inches.

_____

1. $9{,}000 \times 0.001 =$ _____

2. Rewrite this expression using the distributive property.

$$4 \times (8 + m)$$

_____

3. Write 278.2 in word form.

_____

4. Find the area of this parallelogram.

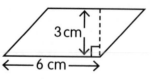

_____

5. What is the ratio of *w*'s to consonants in this sentence?

Wes and Willow went walking.

_____

EMC 754 • © Evan-Moor Corp.

1. 734 + 821 + 486 + 999 = _____

2.   0.1
   x 0.01

3. Round 87.3945 to the nearest hundredth.

   _____

4. What is the perimeter of this figure?

   _____

   31 feet

5. When the queen counted her jewels, she found that she had five pearls for each diamond, two opals and three rubies for each diamond, and two emeralds for each opal. If she has three diamonds, how many jewels does she have altogether?

   _____

1. $\frac{1}{2}$ of 724 = _____

2. $\frac{9}{10}$

    $\frac{9}{100}$

   + 9

3. List all the factors of 21.

   _____

4. Write the next two numbers in this sequence.

   $\frac{1}{2}$ $\frac{1}{4}$ $\frac{1}{8}$ _____   _____

5. If Susie has 7 coins that total 68 cents, what are the coins?

   _____

   _____

Friday ⟨30⟩

Cristy has ten pets including cats, birds, and hamsters. She has twice as many hamsters as cats. Together, her pets have a total of thirty-eight legs. How many of each kind of pet does she have?

Show your work here.

Write your answer here.

Daily Math Practice

Daily Progress Record ⟨30⟩

How many did you get correct each day? Color the squares.

	Monday	Tuesday	Wednesday	Thursday	Friday
5					
4					
3					
2					
1					

 EMC 754 • © Evan-Moor Corp.

1. $0.06 \times 2 =$ _____

2. $88\overline{)1{,}144}$

3. $169 : 13 :: 36 :$ _____

4. What is 5% of 240?

_____

5. Bryan mows lawns after school. He is paid $15 a lawn. If he mows seven lawns a week, how many weeks will he have to work to earn $1,000?

_____

1. $542.472 \div 84 =$ _____

2. $\begin{array}{r} \$98.89 \\ \times \quad 62 \\ \hline \end{array}$

3. Solve for x.

$$16x = 4$$

_____

4. What is the measurement of the fourth angle of a quadrilateral if the others measure 60°, 120°, and 90°?

_____

5. If Pedro needs nine hours of sleep and has to be up at 5:30 A.M., at what time should he go to bed?

_____

1. $20^2 =$ _____

2. $\begin{array}{r} ^-14 \\ + \ ^-7 \\ \hline \end{array}$

3. Define an obtuse angle.

_____

_____

_____

4. In the number 98.713, what digit is in the tenths place?

_____

5. Doug caught two trout weighing two pounds each, one sunfish weighing eight ounces, and a catfish weighing twelve ounces. What is the average weight of the fish that he caught?

_____

Daily Math Practice

Thursday ⟨31⟩

1. $7.5 \div 5 =$ _____

2. $\begin{array}{r} 3\frac{5}{7} \\ + \ 9 \\ \hline \end{array}$

3. A line is perpendicular to another line when the lines intersect at right angles.

true   false

4. How much carpet should Stacey order if her room measures ten feet by twelve feet?

_____

5. The number is a two-digit number. It is odd. The sum of the digits is ten. It is greater than thirty, but less than fifty. What is the number?

_____

  EMC 754 • © Evan-Moor Corp.

Friday 31

Complete the number crossword. Use one numeral, 0 through 9, in each square. The sum of the numbers in the squares must equal the clue. No digits can be repeated within an answer.

CLUES

Across	Down
1. 15	1. 8
3. 14	2. 21
5. 13	3. 16
7. 17	4. 19
9. 13	6. 20
10. 9	8. 10
11. 19	9. 11
13. 20	12. 15

(number crossword grid)

Row 1: [1] 7 | [2] | ■ | [3] 5 | | [4]
Row 2: [5] | 3 | [6] | | ■ |
Row 3: ■ | [7] | | | [8] | 0
Row 4: [9] | | | ■ | [10] |
Row 5: | ■ | [11] 6 | [12] | |
Row 6: [13] 6 | | | 7 | ■ |

Daily Math Practice

Daily Progress Record 31

How many did you get correct each day? Color the squares.

	Monday	Tuesday	Wednesday	Thursday	Friday
5					
4					
3					
2					
1					

1. $126 \times 67 = $ _____

2.　　$\frac{5}{6}$
　　$+ \frac{3}{8}$
　　_____

3. The numbers 48 and 63 have two common factors. What are they?

_____

4. $\frac{3}{8}$ of 16 = _____

5. John gave his friend Sam $\frac{1}{4}$ of his marbles. Sam lost three marbles, so he only has five. How many marbles did John have to start with?

_____

1. $^-4 + 5 = $ _____

2.　　$3\frac{1}{8}$
　　$+ 1\frac{1}{4}$
　　_____

3. What three numbers come next in this pattern?

31　5　32　10　33　15　_____　_____　_____

4. Circle the one number that is incorrect in this solution.

$$\begin{array}{r} 1{,}392 \\ \times\quad 37 \\ \hline 9744 \\ 4176 \\ \hline 50{,}504 \end{array}$$

5. Tonya swims on a relay team with three other swimmers. If each person swims two lengths of the 100-yard pool, how many times would the team have to swim the relay before they swim a mile? (one mile = 5,280 feet)

_____

　　　EMC 754 • © Evan-Moor Corp.

Wednesday ⟨32⟩

1. 348.54 ÷ 37 = _____

2.   3.21
    x 1.07

3. List the factors of 32.

_____

4. Reduce $\frac{51}{57}$ to lowest terms.

_____

5. Steve ran a half-marathon (13 miles). If he completed the race in one hour and forty-four minutes, what was his average time for each mile?

_____

Thursday ⟨32⟩

1. 100^2 = _____

2.   0.32
    1.76
  + 27.02

3. 60% of 54 = _____

4. What is the area of this triangle?

17 cm

8 cm

_____

5. Chloe the cat uses a 5-pound bag of kitty litter every two weeks. If her owners buy a 5-kilogram bag, about how long will it last? (1 kg = approximately 2.2 lbs)

_____

Friday 32

Dave's garden produces six bushels of zucchini, three bushels of beans, seven bushels of corn, and four bushels of beets. Organize this information into a table. Tell what percentage and fraction of Dave's total crop each vegetable represents.

Show your work here.

Write your answer here.

Daily Math Practice

Daily Progress Record 32

How many did you get correct each day? Color the squares.

	Monday	Tuesday	Wednesday	Thursday	Friday
5					
4					
3					
2					
1					

EMC 754 • © Evan-Moor Corp.

1. 96.240 ÷ 2 = _____

2.   0.030
     x 0.002

3. Johan asked for two triple-dip cones. If each scoop is 55 cents, how much will he pay?

_____

4. Lines AB and CD are

_____.

5. Lines CD and EF are

_____.

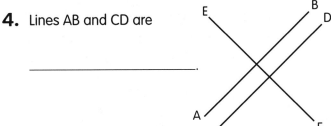

1. $1\frac{1}{4} \times 3\frac{1}{2}$ = _____

2.   0.30
     x   75

3. Reduce $\frac{36}{144}$ to lowest terms.

_____

4.

Angle CAB is an _____ angle.

5. Zaid will travel from Boston to Washington, D.C. If the trip is 600 miles, about how fast will he have to go to get there in $10\frac{1}{2}$ hours?

_____

1. 72,649 + 7,129 = _____

2.
```
  36,000
−    982
```

3. Add a sign.

8 4 3 5 2 6 7 1 = 5,764

4. Define an equilateral triangle.

_____

_____

_____

5. If each cup of unpopped kernels makes 3 cups of popped corn, how many quarts of popped corn will a 16-ounce bag of kernels make?

_____

1. 654,201 − 98,999 = _____

2. 25⟌37,192

3. Solve for x.

$$0.3x = 2.4$$

_____

4. Which of these is heavier?

◯ one ounce   ◯ ten grams

5. Mrs. Roberts organized her class into four equal-sized teams. Boys make up $\frac{3}{4}$ of each of the teams. If there are 2 girls on each team, how many students are there in the whole class?

_____

EMC 754 • © Evan-Moor Corp.

Find the missing numbers. (Each shape stands for one number.)

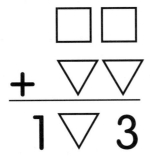

Daily Math Practice

Daily Progress Record 〈33〉

How many did you get correct each day? Color the squares.

	Monday	Tuesday	Wednesday	Thursday	Friday
5					
4					
3					
2					
1					

1. 0.021 x 7.3 = _____

2.   765,945
       + 282,067

3. Name two shapes that always have only two sets of parallel sides.

_____

4. Round 967,727.96 to the nearest hundred thousand.

_____

5. Write a word problem with the answer of 26 that uses at least two different math operations.

_____

_____

_____

_____

_____

---

1. $\frac{1}{4}$ x 640 = _____

2. 43)‾28,036‾

3. The baseball game started at 2:15 P.M. and ran 2 hours and 48 minutes. At what time did the game end?

_____

4. What is the range of this data?

6.2, 8.1, 7.4, 3.5

_____

5. If Starvos orders a pizza for $5.99, a soda for $1.50, and breadsticks for $2.49, and hands $10.00 to the cashier, how much change will he receive?

_____

    EMC 754 • © Evan-Moor Corp.

Wednesday 34

1. $\frac{3}{9} \div \frac{1}{9} =$ _____

2. 76,321
   x 3,748

3. What is the measurement of the third angle of a triangle if the first two angles measure 45 degrees and 71 degrees?

   _____

4. Place the following numbers on the number line and label them.

   $^-1, ^-2\frac{1}{2}, \frac{3}{4}$

5. Farmer Ed has 500 cattle in the pasture. When he rides his horse into the pasture to sort the cattle, how many legs are in the pasture?

   _____

Daily Math Practice

Thursday 34

1. $50^2 =$ _____

2. $^-2$
   $+ ^-6$

3. How many inches are in 6 feet?

   _____

   in 6 yards?

   _____

4. $\frac{1}{4} : \frac{3}{4} :: 75 :$ _____

5. Popeye the parrot sings five different notes—F, C, D, E-flat, and G. Write 10 different tunes that he can sing. Each tune must be six notes long and include all five notes.

   _____

   _____

   _____

   _____

   _____

Friday ⟨34⟩

Mrs. Shelton doesn't have enough marking pens for everyone in class. Every two students share a green pen and every four students share a red pen. If she has 15 marking pens in all, how many students are in Mrs. Shelton's class?

Show your work here.

Write your answer here.

Daily Progress Record ⟨34⟩

How many did you get correct each day? Color the squares.

	Monday	Tuesday	Wednesday	Thursday	Friday
5					
4					
3					
2					
1					

EMC 754 • © Evan-Moor Corp.

1. $6.17 \div 2 =$ _____

2. $9\frac{4}{5}$
$+ 3\frac{2}{3}$

3. Which of these is the best estimate of a new pencil's length?

   ○ 7 cm   ○ 17 cm   ○ 170 cm

4. Write 67.92 in word form.

_____

5. If Jason ran 2 miles and Josh ran 3,000 yards, who ran the farthest? (There are 5,280 feet in a mile.)

_____

---

1. $(3 - 4) + 6 =$ _____

2. Correct this problem.   2,964

   + 1,043
   3,907

3. How many quarts are in six gallons?

_____

4. What is the smallest fraction you can write using the digits 6, 7, and 1?

_____

5. In a bag, there are three brown candies, six red candies, four yellow candies, and one blue candy. Without looking, what is the chance of choosing a yellow candy?

_____

1. 0.002 x 3.5 = _____

2. Use the distributive property to rewrite this expression.

3 (4 + n)

_____

3. What is the perimeter of this figure?

6 cm

_____

4. Find the area of this figure.

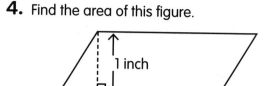

1 inch

←— 2 inches —→

_____

5. Bubble gum comes in packs of 7 pieces and cases of 48 packs. If Tara needs 7,500 pieces for the carnival, how many cases should she order?

_____

1. 6.43 – 0.5 = _____

2.   67,432
   35,978
+ 4,721

3. Define *congruent*.

_____

_____

_____

4. Solve for *x*.

7x = 42

_____

5. What is the ratio of *s*'s to all of the letters in this phrase?

She sold six sea stars.

_____

EMC 754 • © Evan-Moor Corp.

Graph and label these coordinate pairs.
Then name points E, F, G, and H using
correct ordered pair notation.

A (3, 1)
B (4, 6)
C (⁻2, 3)
D (⁻5, 2)

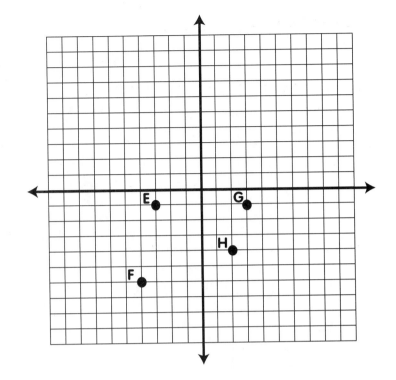

Daily Progress Record 〈**35**〉

How many did you get correct each day? Color the squares.

	Monday	Tuesday	Wednesday	Thursday	Friday
5					
4					
3					
2					
1					

1. $9.23 \div 071 =$ _____

2. $\begin{array}{r} 9.23 \\ + 0.071 \\ \hline \end{array}$

3. What is 4^3?

_____

4. Fill in the missing numbers.

_____   9 11 33 35 105 107 _____

5. If there are sixty-four knives, forks, and spoons on the table and each place setting has two forks, how many places are set?

_____

---

1. $296 \times 304 =$ _____

2. $15\overline{)2,100}$

3. $\frac{4}{7} - \frac{1}{2} =$ _____

4. What is the area of this figure?

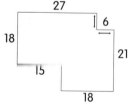

5. If each person at a picnic drinks 710 milliliters of soda, how many liter bottles are needed for 10 people?

_____

1. $7\frac{3}{8} - 2\frac{1}{4} = $ _____

2. 74.19
     – 62.04

3. Mark the fractions that are expressed in lowest terms.

$$\frac{19}{77} \qquad \frac{34}{51} \qquad \frac{8}{13} \qquad \frac{16}{48} \qquad \frac{28}{112}$$

4. How many cups are in a gallon?

_____

5. Show six ways to name or describe the number 81.

1. $5\overline{)11.35}$

2. 4.03
     x 2.71

3.

●————————————●
A   B

$\overline{AB}$ is a _____.

4. How many milliliters are in one liter?

a. 10   d. 1,000

b. 500   e. 5,000

c. 100

5. Write a question to match this answer:

6 boxes of 12

_____

_____

_____

Create equations for numerals, **using four and only four 5's**. See how many numerals 1 through 10 you can do. Add decimal points, parentheses, +, −, ×, ÷.

Example: $1 = \dfrac{5 - 5 + 5}{5}$

1 = _____   6 = _____

2 = _____   7 = _____

3 = _____   8 = _____

4 = _____   9 = _____

5 = _____   10 = _____

Daily Progress Record ⬡36⬡

How many did you get correct each day? Color the squares.

	Monday	Tuesday	Wednesday	Thursday	Friday
5					
4					
3					
2					
1					

EMC 754 • © Evan-Moor Corp.

How to Solve
Word Problems

 Read the problem carefully. Think about what it says.

 Look for clue words. The clue words will tell you which operation to use—addition, subtraction, multiplication, or division. Hint: Sometimes you will use more than one operation.

 Solve the problem.

 Check your work. Make sure your answer makes sense.

Clue Words

Add	Subtract	Multiply	Divide
in all	how much more	times	parts
altogether	more than	product of	equal parts
total	less than	multiplied by	separated
sum	are left	by (with measurements or dimensions)	divided by
both	take away		quotient of
plus	difference	area	a fraction of
	fewer		average

EMC 754 • © Evan-Moor Corp.

EMC 754 • © Evan-Moor Corp.

Monday
1. 68
2. 116
3. 3 m, 3 cm, 3 mm
4. 8 P.M.
5. 24 cups

Tuesday
1. 39
2. 223
3. 5,300
4. A square is a quadrilateral with equal sides and equal angles.
5. 13 pounds of peanuts

Wednesday
1. 56
2. 18
3. 50 degrees
4. 1 in 3 or $\frac{1}{3}$
5. 7

Thursday
1. 9
2. 7
3. 3,617
4. 7
5. $1

Friday
Examples will vary. The final answer is always 22!

Monday
1. 91
2. 162
3. 60 inches
4. ⬭
5. Wilbur was 36. Orville was 32. Wilbur was 4 years older.

Tuesday
1. 49
2. 163
3.

Subjects	Hands
1	2
2	4
3	6
4	8
5	10
10	20
15	30

4. Answers should be multiples of 2 and 3 (e.g., 6, 12, 18, 24, etc.).
5. 92 million kilometers

Wednesday
1. 45
2. 24
3. 352, 176, 704
4. 1, 2, 7, 14—1, 2, and 7 should be circled.
5. 24 packs

Thursday
1. 7
2. 5
3. ten-thousands
4. < (less than)
5. $54

Friday

$\frac{1}{4}$	$1\frac{1}{4}$	1
$1\frac{7}{12}$	$\frac{5}{6}$	$\frac{1}{12}$
$\frac{2}{3}$	$\frac{5}{12}$	$1\frac{5}{12}$

Monday
1. 96
2. 813
3. 32"
4. 52°F
5. $1.83

Tuesday
1. 395
2. 69
3.

Wednesday
1. 15
2. 28
3. 8
4. Bert has to mow half of the lawn.
5. 14 cups, 182 pretzels

Thursday
1. 7
2. 5
3. a liter
4. 6
5. 36 months

4. Answers will vary. Possible answers might include: tablet, eraser, pencil box, or calculator.
5. 735 people

Friday
Rule: divide by 2 and add 4

Input	Output
12	10
24	16
32	20
62	35
70	39
86	47

Week 4

Monday
1. 75
2. 6,663
3. 3,743; 7,660
4. 5
5. 12 players

Tuesday
1. 68
2. 96
3. ◆ ▼ ▼ ●
4. The decimal point divides the whole from the parts, the dollars from the cents.
5. 9

Wednesday
1. 40
2. 48
3. 9 + 7 = 16, 7 + 9 = 16, 16 − 9 = 7, 16 − 7 = 9
4. thousand
5. 108 balls were pitched, 72 balls were hit

Thursday
1. 9
2. 17
3. 4
4. 12,020
5. $378

Friday
147 square feet

Week 5

Monday
1. 89
2. 15,409
3. 2 P.M.
4. y = 9
5. 600 pies

Tuesday
1. 135
2. 439
3.
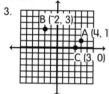

4. 4 cups
5. Ted should use the formula for finding the area of a right triangle—$\frac{1}{2}$ the base x the height. His patio has an area of 63 square units.

Wednesday
1. 63
2. 12.8
3. 4 x 4 x 4 = 64
4. =
5. 29 South American birds

Thursday
1. 4
2. 5
3. 1, 2, 3, 6
4. seven hundred five
5. more—by 42,116 kilometers

Friday
with 3 digits = 1,089; with 4 digits = 10,890
The answer for 4 digits was 10 times the answer for 3 digits. Predictions for 5 digits will vary, but students will discover that the pattern changes to 109,890.

Week 6

Monday
1. 287
2. 728
3. < (less than)
4. 1, 2, 5, 10
5. $38.83

Tuesday
1. 624
2. 369
3. one hundred thirty-two
4. tenths
5. 5 crates

Wednesday
1. 27
2. 450
3. 9, 11, 12
4. B
5. 12:10 P.M.

Thursday
1. 7
2. 43
3. 1 inch, 10 inches, 1 foot, 1 yard, 10 feet
4. A, D, E
5. 15 minutes

Friday
6 dimes, 4 nickels, 20 pennies

Explanation:
Since two-fifteenths of the coins are nickels, the total number of coins must be a multiple of 15 (15, 30, 45, 60, etc.).

Convert the other 2 fractions to fifteenths: 1/5 = 3/15; 2/3 = 10/15.

Then create a grid to help you find which multiple of 15 will yield $1.00.

Possible # of Coins	Dimes = 3/15 of total	Nickels = 2/15 of total	Pennies = 10/15 of total	Money Amount
15	3 dimes = 30¢	2 nickels = 10¢	10 pennies = 10¢	30 + 10 + 10 = 50¢ Not correct
30	6 dimes = 60¢	4 nickels = 20¢	20 pennies = 20¢	60 + 20 + 20 = $1.00 **Correct**
45	No need to do this			

118

EMC 754 • © Evan-Moor Corp.

Week 7

Monday
1. 992
2. 154.09
3. 4, 8, 12
4. 6,800
5. 72 pieces of candy

Tuesday
1. 1,207
2. 174
3. Graphs will vary.
4. 573
5. 7 cups

Wednesday
1. 42
2. 75
3. 38
4. 1 ounce, 10 ounces, 1 pound
5. Peg—by 1 cent

Thursday
1. 3
2. 8
3. 157
4. 22.5 sq. cm
5. 372 pounds

Friday
Mrs. Sage will need two reams of paper (980 sheets).

Week 8

Monday
1. 826
2. 9,773
3. 37
4. 18
5. Eva is 51" tall. Luis is 39" tall.

Tuesday
1. 2.5
2. $\frac{1}{2}$
3. 10 cm
4. 4 sq. cm
5. $4.16

Wednesday
1. 24
2. 68
3. The quotient is the answer in a division problem.
4. 12 in.
5. 1 out of 3 or $\frac{1}{3}$; 1 out of 4 or $\frac{1}{4}$

Thursday
1. 19
2. 40
3. ●▼◆●▼
4. 1 and 5
5. a rectangular prism

Friday
Although the boxes are different sizes, they have the same volume—750 cubic inches.

Week 9

Monday
1. 11.2
2. 1,223
3. The number has a 5 or a 0 in the ones place.
4. 4,379,800
5. 24 crackers

Tuesday
1. 21.62
2. 3,476
3. A $\frac{3}{8}$, B 1$\frac{1}{8}$
4. 42
5. 16 posts

Wednesday
1. 56
2. 36.4
3. 71
4. c
5. 40 popcorn balls

Thursday
1. 46
2. 128
3. 184 square inches
4. 2
5. 23 votes

Friday
a parallelogram

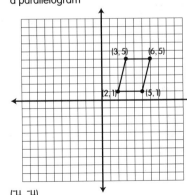

Monday
1. 6
2. 1,770
3. 30
4. 50%
5.

Tuesday
1. $3\frac{1}{2}$
2. 378
3. 8
4. 1 in 3 or $\frac{1}{3}$
5. 62

Wednesday
1. $2\frac{1}{2}$ or 2.5
2. 74.34
3. 10,040
4. 25, 36, 49—The output is the input squared.
5. 20 cents

Thursday
1. 0.2
2. 25
3. 10, 5
4. 40 sq. in.
5. 12 boys, 6 girls

Friday

Boxes	Faces
3	13
5	21
11	45

Rule: 4 x (# of boxes) + 1

Monday
1. 14.8
2. 16,611
3. 3 and 7
4. a right angle, a 90-degree angle
5. $\frac{1}{5}$, 20%

Tuesday
1. 5.7
2. 364
3. > (more than)
4. ten-thousands
5. $63\frac{1}{2}$ inches or 5 foot $3\frac{1}{2}$ inches

Wednesday
1. $\frac{1}{12}$
2. 4,480
3. 6
4. 116.6
5. $37.50, $18.75 each**Thursday**
1. 0.7
2. 82
3. A $-\frac{3}{4}$ B $\frac{1}{4}$
4. 10, 10
5. Buy-Here is a better buy. The gummi worms are 70 cents per pound less than at Save-More.

Friday

Total attendance = 219,000

Monday
1. $1\frac{1}{12}$
2. 1,110
3. A and C
4. six thousand, three hundred fifty-two and eight tenths
5. $12.99

Tuesday
1. 38.67
2. $3\frac{1}{2}$
3. 32 cubic inches
4. 3
5. 41 degrees

Wednesday
1. 22,710
2. 8.97
3. 1 P.M.
4. 5, 5, 6
5. 99 square yards; $1,583.01

Thursday
1. $\frac{1}{2}$
2. 0.53
3. 2
4.
5. $\frac{3}{5}$ walk home, $\frac{1}{5}$ ride the bus

Friday
10 different combinations

EMC 754 • © Evan-Moor Corp.

Monday
1. 6.3
2. 4,404
3. a cube
4. 2, 59, 5
5. about 5 liters

Tuesday
1. 132
2. $\frac{5}{8}$
3. 45,366
4. diameter–bd, center–a, radius–ca
5. $310.86

Wednesday
1. 1,152
2. $4\frac{1}{2}$
3. 13
4. 128; 512; 2,048
5. 27 plants

Thursday
1. $\frac{2}{5}$
2. 34
3. $\frac{3}{4}$
4. 18
5. 35 students

Friday

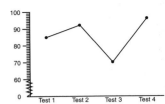

Monday
1. 77
2. $1\frac{2}{9}$
3. 895,000,000
4. square
5. $12.50

Tuesday
1. $2\frac{1}{2}$
2. 9,953
3. Answers will vary. One possible answer:
   The answer would have 5 digits.
4. 42
5. Marie–100, Misu–99, Tala–92, Kane–86

Wednesday
1. 0.13581
2. $\frac{9}{50}$
3. 54 square inches
4. 7
5. Monday, Thursday, and Saturday

Thursday
1. $1\frac{1}{8}$
2. 7.35
3. 26
4. A square is a quadrilateral with two pairs of equal
   parallel sides and four equal angles.
5. $7.50

Friday
The Baby Cup is the best buy.

Monday
1. 12,586
2. 14,809
3. 9,820
4. hexagon
5. 39 mph

Tuesday
1. $1\frac{1}{4}$
2. 93,471
3. 1, 2, 4, 7, 14, 28
4. 2, 3, 5
5. 28'

Wednesday
1. 15,459.12
2. $\frac{3}{32}$
3. 64 ounces
4. 0.06
5. 400 centimeters

Thursday
1. 0.5
2. 1,314.7
3. Fill the 3-cup container and pour it into the 5-cup
   container. Fill the 3-cup container again. Pour it into
   the 5-cup container until the container is full. There
   is 1 cup left in the 3-cup container.
4. A circle is a closed figure in which every point on the
   circumference is equidistant from the center point.
5. 15 marbles

Friday
Graphs will vary.

Monday
1. 142
2. 766,871
3. The high temperature on Monday was below the average weekly high temperature.
4. $a = 8$
5. $7.73—Combinations of coins and bills will vary.

Tuesday
1. 37,335
2. 3.68
3. perimeter = 28 cm, area = 22 square cm
4. $\frac{7}{8}$
5. 1,080 hours

Wednesday
1. 3.552
2. $\frac{3}{7}$
3. false
4. 6
5. $\frac{5}{8}$ of the pizza was left.

Thursday
1. 2
2. 0.61
3. Drawings will vary, but should show an angle greater than 90°.
4. 45,366
5. 24 students

Friday
90 kilograms of sand

Monday
1. $7\frac{1}{2}$
2. 9,342
3. 369.228
4. A perimeter is the distance around a closed figure.
5. 24 red tulip bulbs, 48 yellow tulip bulbs, and 24 white tulip bulbs

Tuesday
1. 97,236
2. $8\frac{3}{5}$
3. 3
4. 10, 20, 18
5. $1\frac{1}{2}$ or 1.5 gallons a day

Wednesday
1. 1,876.16
2. 4.17
3. 0.791, 7.19, 17.9, 91.7, 197, 971
4. true
5. about $11\frac{1}{2}$ weeks

Thursday
1. $6\frac{3}{4}$
2. 365
3. 49
4. Drawings should show an angle of 90°.
5. about 3 hours

Friday
8 posts, 64 feet of chicken wire

Monday
1. 1,237
2. $476.22
3. 18 inches
4. 512
5. 42,225 tickets sold; 275 others

Tuesday
1. 4,554
2. $24.01
3. $z = 1$
4. about 6 inches
5. 21 sit-ups per minute

Wednesday
1. 69,969
2. 0.15
3. Illustrations will vary.
4. 24
5. $12

Thursday
1. $3\frac{1}{2}$
2. 8,203
3. 11
4. 8, 7
5. The gallon is the better buy.

Friday
One solution:
$1 + 9 = 10$, $6 + 2 = 8$, $7 + 5 = 12$, $4 + 3 = 7$

EMC 754 • © Evan-Moor Corp.

Monday
1. 85.27
2. 4,129
3. 1, 2, 3, 4, 6, 8, 12, 24
4. 24 + 61 + 3 = 88
5. a cube

Tuesday
1. $\frac{7}{10}$
2. 6.3
3. 48 ounces
4. four thousand, eight hundred one
5. $\frac{2}{3}$

Wednesday
1. 34
2. $\frac{29}{40}$
3. $\frac{6}{7}$
4. no—

```
      461,592
   x      308
      3592736
     1394 7760
   142 070336
```

○ = First mistake
□ + also a mistake

5. 3 place mats

Thursday
1. 1.335
2. 357,000
3. 42
4. 14
5. 100 on the grass, 200 in chairs, and 300 sat in the bleachers

Friday

	Blue	Green	Pink	White
James	x	x	x	○
May	x	x	○	x
Brett	○	x	x	x
Elisa	x	○	x	x

Monday
1. 144
2. 39.9
3. seventy-five and nine-tenths
4. 7
5. 12 cups

Tuesday
1. 0.8
2. 1
3. 152
4. 300
5. 4 pounds, 2 ounces

Wednesday
1. 4,033
2. $6\frac{11}{12}$
3. 10
4. 1 cubic inch
5. $\frac{1}{6}$

Thursday
1. 41.6
2. $6\frac{3}{20}$
3. > (more than)
4. 18
5. $24

Friday

Points shown: (-2, 4), (6, 4), (2, 0), (-2, -4), (6, -4)

(2, 0) is the center point.

Monday
1. 74
2. 224,208
3. 205
4. The number is divided by ten to create the next number in the sequence.
5. yes

Tuesday
1. 1
2. 217.35
3. 0
4. 92,200
5. 250 seconds, a little more than 4 minutes

Wednesday
1. 7.78
2. ⁻39
3. about 5,000—Explanations will vary.
4. 8
5. 3 quarters, 1 dime, 1 nickel, 1 penny or 1 half-dollar, 4 dimes, 1 penny

Thursday
1. 932,291
2. 460,718
3. fifty-seven and three tenths
4. 1, 2, 4, 8, 16
5. 5 pages

Friday
Titles will vary.

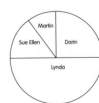

Lynda $\frac{1}{2}$
Darin $\frac{1}{4}$

Monday
1. 1,237
2. 3,218
3. 0.800, 0.83, 8.00, 8.30
4. x = 182
5. $2

Tuesday
1. 54
2. $2.29
3. ⁻6 degrees
4.
5. Jorge is 11 years old.

Wednesday
1. $1\frac{1}{14}$
2. $\frac{3}{5}$
3. 2
4. thousandths
5. about 800 words

Thursday
1. $1\frac{3}{4}$
2. 4,673
3. 42
4. 21 feet, 252 inches
5. 6 ways

Friday
One possible answer:

16	12	32
36	20	4
8	28	24

Monday
1. 507
2. $1\frac{3}{8}$
3. x = 14
4. pentagon
5. Six bikes are black, two are silver, and four are other colors.

Tuesday
1. 0.2
2. 27
3. 6,000.01
4. 9.1
5. 30 seconds

Wednesday
1. 291.88
2. $\frac{23}{24}$
3. 3.27
4. 1, 2
5. 768 pretzels

Thursday
1. 0.3
2. 131,400
3. 3 eggs
4. 16 in.
5. 16 jars

Friday
13.10 km

Monday
1. 0.48
2. 13
3. 364 x 20 = 7,280
4. Answers will vary, but should include regrouping to get more ones and then again to get more tens.
5. 35

Tuesday
1. 49
2. $\frac{7}{12}$
3. 8
4. 12 sq cm
5. $858

Wednesday
1. ⁻8
2. 0.3996
3. 26, 46
4. b = 4
5. $36

Thursday
1. 27
2. $1\frac{3}{5}$
3. 10 grams
4. 20
5. 85 questions

Friday
36 mammals, 8 reptiles, 4 birds

EMC 754 • © Evan-Moor Corp.

Monday
1. 1,000
2. 16
3. 1
4. 10 grams
5. $21

Tuesday
1. ⁻5
2. ⁻7
3. Answers will vary, but should include mixed numbers.
4. 94, 87
5. 0.32 inches of rain

Wednesday
1. $\frac{2}{15}$
2. $4\frac{7}{12}$
3. true
4. 75
5. 5'

Thursday
1. 3
2. ⁻7
3. 88,900
4. 1, 2, 3, 6, 9, 18
5. 10 games

Friday

```
        [36]
      [20][16]
    [12][8][8]
  [7][5][3][5]
```

Monday
1. 15
2. 64
3. 2.1
4. 24.375 square feet
5. 20 cones, 10 balls

Tuesday
1. $6\frac{13}{15}$
2. 12
3. A and B
4.

Input	Output
1	12
2	14
3	16

5. 24%

Wednesday
1. 34,354,772
2. $1.53
3. $b = 27$
4. $1\frac{5}{6}$
5. The parking lot is $\frac{4}{5}$ full. When Mrs. Johnson parks, the fraction gets bigger—$\frac{5}{6}$.

Thursday
1. 4.68
2. ⁻3
3. about 6,000
4. acute angles
5. 3 quarters, 3 dimes, 1 nickel

Friday
48, 91, 82, 76, 64

Monday
1. 5,784
2. $17,766.23
3. $29.04
4. a cylinder
5. 11

Tuesday
1. 1.71
2. $\frac{5}{12}$
3. 1
4. true
5. 13 pounds, 2 ounces

Wednesday
1. 296,759
2. 2.718
3. 1, 0.1
4. a cylindrical prism
5. 3

Thursday
1. 7,166
2. 51
3. a rectangular prism
4. 8, 16, 24, 32, 40, 48, 56, 64, 72, 80, 88, 96
5. total = 4 hours, 10 minutes
   average = 50 minutes

Friday

```
    (4)           (32)
      (12)  (24)
        (20)
      (16)  (28)
  (8)           (36)
```

Monday
1. 11.56
2. 14,687
   − 9,781
   4,906
3. 1, 2, 4, 7, 14, 28—1, 2, and 7 should be circled.
4. 398,670
5. $45.05

Tuesday
1. 4.88   4. 92, 78
2. 18   5. 26 cups
3. 5,280,000

Wednesday
1. 31
2. ⁻6
3. 1, 7
4. a hexagon
5. One possible answer:

⑧
②⑥⑩
④

Thursday
1. $\frac{3}{4}$
2. 5.55
3. 43 cm
4. 1
5. $5\frac{1}{2}$ hours

Friday
Shaded boxes form the word good.

Factors of 12	5	11	7	8	11	9	7	13	9	5	7	10	7	3
Factors of 41	3	2	10	4	11	5	7	6	12	18	9	18	3	2	1
Factors of 60	60	1	5	7	2	12	4	8	3	15	10	9	20	6	30
Factors of 48	3	5	12	9	24	7	4	11	16	11	48	10	1	13	2
Factors of 72	36	12	72	5	4	3	6	7	18	24	8	9	2	1
Factors of 19	2	3	19	4	7	11	5	10	5	6	12	9	13	8	8
Factors of 16	5	3	2	7	13	3	10	14	6	15	5	11	9	12	6
Factors of 24	3	2	8	5	7	9	13	5	14	11	19	5	10	7

Monday
1. 81
2. $8\frac{7}{20}$
3. $x = 35$
4. 6,400,006.6
5. 35 minutes

Tuesday
1. $1\frac{2}{7}$
2. 0.075
3. 4 A.M. on Tuesday
4. 45 feet
5. dinner = $\frac{1}{2}$ hour, television = 1 hour,
   homework = 3 hours, gymnastics = 2 hours,
   piano = 1 hour

Wednesday
1. ⁻12
2. 13,526.19
3. 3
4. 90 degrees
5. 10 ounces

Thursday
1. ⁻8
2. $3\frac{1}{3}$
3. 658 × 12 = 7,896
4. 4, 88
5. 200

Friday

Cube A: is opposite

Cube B: is opposite

Monday
1. 225
2. 0.34
3. $\frac{2}{43}$
4. 20 cups
5. 4' 2"

Tuesday
1. 9
2. 4 × 8 + 4 × m or 32 + 4m
3. two hundred seventy-eight and two-tenths
4. 18 sq. cm **OR** 4×3
                    +
                 3×2
5. $\frac{5}{16}$

Wednesday
1. 3,040
2. 0.001
3. 87.39
4. 155 feet
5. 45 jewels

Thursday
1. 362
2. $9\frac{99}{100}$
3. 1, 3, 7, 21
4. $\frac{1}{16}$, $\frac{1}{32}$
5. 2 quarters, 1 dime, 1 nickel, 3 pennies or
   1 half-dollar, 3 nickels, 3 pennies

Friday
6 hamsters, 3 cats, and 1 bird

EMC 754 • © Evan-Moor Corp.

Monday
1. 0.12
2. 13
3. 6
4. 12
5. In 10 weeks, he will have earned $1,050.

Tuesday
1. 6.458
2. $6,131.18
3. $x = \frac{1}{4}$
4. 90°
5. 8:30 P.M.

Wednesday
1. 400
2. ⁻21
3. An obtuse angle is any angle greater than 90 degrees.
4. 7
5. 1 lb. 5 oz.

Thursday
1. 1.5
2. $12\frac{5}{7}$
3. true
4. 120 square feet
5. 37

Friday
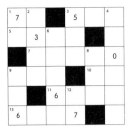

Monday
1. 8,442
2. $1\frac{5}{24}$
3. 1 and 3
4. 6
5. 32 marbles

Tuesday
1. 1
2. $4\frac{3}{8}$
3. 34, 20, 35
4.
$$\begin{array}{r} 1393 \\ \times\ 37 \\ \hline 9744 \\ 4176 \\ \hline 50504 \end{array}$$
5. After three relays, the team will have swum over a mile.

Wednesday
1. 9.42
2. 3.4347
3. 1, 2, 4, 8, 16, 32
4. $\frac{17}{19}$
5. 8 minutes per mile

Thursday
1. 10,000
2. 29.1
3. 32.4
4. 68 sq. cm
5. about 4 weeks

Friday
30% zucchini, 15% beans, 35% corn, 20% beets

$\frac{3}{10}$ $\frac{3}{20}$ $\frac{9}{20}$ $\frac{1}{5}$

vegetable	number
zucchini	6
beans	3
corn	7
beets	4

Monday
1. 48.12
2. 0.00006
3. $3.30
4. parallel
5. perpendicular

Tuesday
1. $4\frac{3}{8}$
2. 22.5
3. $\frac{1}{4}$
4. acute
5. just over 57 miles per hour

Wednesday
1. 79,778
2. 35,018
3. 8,435 − 2,671 = 5,764
4. An equilateral triangle has three equal angles and three equal sides.
5. $1\frac{1}{2}$ quarts

Thursday
1. 555,202
2. 1,487.68
3. 8
4. one ounce
5. 32 students

Friday
$$\begin{array}{r} 99 \\ +\ 44 \\ \hline 143 \end{array}$$

Monday
1. 0.1533
2. 1,048,012
3. Answers should include rectangle, square, parallelogram, and/or rhombus.
4. 1,000,000
5. Problems will vary.

Tuesday
1. 160
2. 652
3. 5:03 P.M.
4. 4.6
5. 2 cents

Wednesday
1. 3
2. 286,051,108
3. 64
4.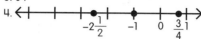
5. 2,006 legs

Thursday
1. 2,500
2. ⁻8
3. 72 in., 216 in.
4. 225
5. Tunes will vary.

Friday
20 students

Monday
1. 3.085
2. $13\frac{7}{15}$
3. 17 cm
4. sixty-seven and ninety-two hundredths
5. Jason

Tuesday
1. 5
2. $\begin{array}{r} 2,964 \\ + 1,043 \\ \hline 4,007 \end{array}$
3. 24 quarts
4. $\frac{1}{76}$
5. $\frac{2}{7}$ or 2 out of 7

Wednesday
1. 0.007
2. $3 \times 4 + 3 \times n$ or $12 + 3n$
3. 36 cm
4. 2 sq. in.
5. 23 cases

Thursday
1. 5.93
2. 108,131
3. Two things are congruent if they are exactly the same size and shape.
4. $x = 6$
5. $\frac{1}{3}$ or 1 out of 3

Friday
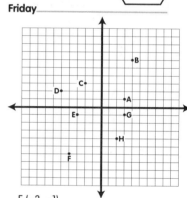
E (−3, −1)
F (−4, −6)
G (3, −1)
H (2, −4)

Monday
1. 0.13
2. 9.301
3. 64
4. 3, 321
5. 16 place settings

Tuesday
1. 89,984
2. 140
3. $\frac{1}{14}$
4. 720 square units
5. 8 liters

Wednesday
1. $5\frac{1}{8}$
2. 12.15
3. $\frac{19}{77}, \frac{8}{13}$
4. 16 cups
5. Answers will vary (e.g., 9 squared, 83 − 2).

Thursday
1. 2.27
2. 10.9213
3. line segment
4. d
5. Answers will vary (e.g., Cody wants to put 72 apples into boxes that can each hold 12 apples. How many boxes can he fill?).

Friday
There are many possible answers, for example:

$$1 = \frac{5 - 5 + 5}{5} \text{ or } 1 = \frac{5}{5} (5 \div 5).$$